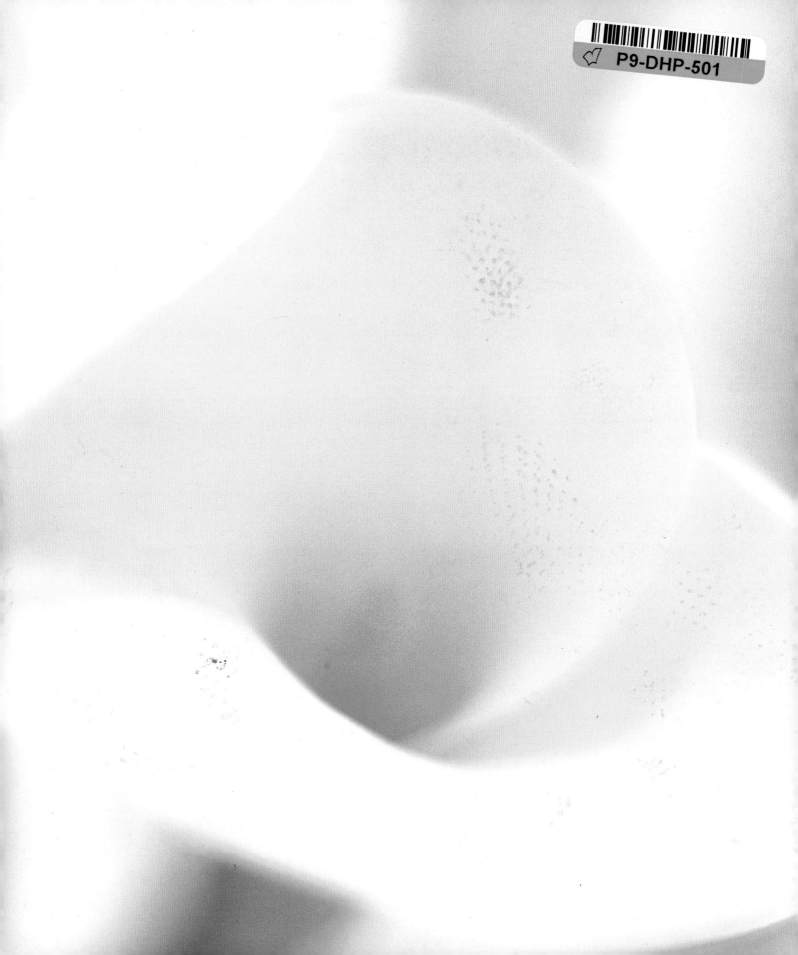

THE
Newlyweds'
COOKBOOK

THE Newlyweds' COOKBOOK

RYLAND
PETERS
& SMALL
LONDON NEW YORK

Designer *Sarah Fraser*

Commissioning Editor *Elsa Petersen-Schepelern*

Editor *Sharon Cochrane*

Picture Research *Emily Westlake*

Production Manager *Patricia Harrington*

Editorial Manager *Julia Charles*

Art Director *Anne-Marie Bulat*

Publishing Director *Alison Starling*

Index *Hilary Bird*

First published in the United States in 2006
by Ryland Peters & Small, Inc.
519 Broadway, 5th Floor
New York, NY 10012
www.rylandpeters.com

10 9 8

Text copyright © Celia Brooks Brown, Maxine Clark,
Linda Collister, Clare Ferguson, Manisha Gambhir Harkins,
Jane Noraika, Louise Pickford, Ben Reed, Sonia Stevenson,
Linda Tubby, Fran Warde, Laura Washburn, Lesley Waters
(recipes previously published in *How to Cook* by Ryland
Peters & Small), and Lindy Wildsmith, 2006
Design and photographs copyright
© Ryland Peters & Small, 2006

Printed in China

Notes

All spoon measurements are level unless otherwise
specified.

All eggs are large unless otherwise specified. Uncooked
or partly cooked eggs should not be served to the very
young, the very old, those with compromised immune
systems, or to pregnant women.

Ovens should be preheated to the specified temperature. If
using a fan-assisted oven, cooking times should be reduced
according to the manufacturer's instructions.

To sterilize preserving jars, wash them in hot, soapy water
and rinse in boiling water. Place in a large saucepan and
cover with hot water. With the saucepan lid on, bring the
water to a boil and continue boiling for 15 minutes. Turn
off the heat and leave the jars in the hot water until just
before they are to be filled. Invert the jars onto a clean
dishtowel to dry. Sterilize the lids for 5 minutes, by boiling,
or according to the manufacturer's instructions. Jars should
be filled and sealed while they are still hot.

Library of Congress Cataloging-in-Publication Data

The Newlyweds' cookbook.
    p. cm.
  Includes index.
  ISBN-13: 978-1-84172-964-0
  ISBN-10: 1-84172-964-7
  1. Cookery.

TX714.N528 2006
641.5--dc22

2005021895

Contents

introduction

Getting married is one of the most exciting moments of your life. After the joys of the day itself, there are the delights of setting up home together. One of the many pleasures of married life is cooking for your loved one or, better still, preparing a meal together. You will no doubt receive a range of wonderful wedding gifts for your new home. For the first time in your lives you might own a decent set of saucepans or fabulous kitchen knives, as well as a complete set of dinner plates and dessert bowls. A well-equipped kitchen is sure to inspire you to cook up some delicious meals for your partner, family, and friends.

This is where *The Newlyweds' Cookbook* comes into its own. It is a delicious source of culinary inspiration for every day of your new married life together. First, Kitchen Basics talks you through all the essential equipment and pantry items you will need in order to put a meal together. Then the recipe chapters cover everything from Brunch to Family Gatherings and Drinks. From quick weekday dinners that can be thrown together at the end of a busy day, to Special Occasions when you want to push the boat out and make something really memorable, this book is packed with ideas.

Sharing a meal with your loved one is an important part of daily life—on busy days, cooking and eating dinner may be the only chance you get to spend some time together and catch up with each other's news. You don't need to prepare a banquet every day, the simplest meal from the Quick Meals chapter can be made special just by eating it together. Cooking for friends and family should be a pleasure, and it can be with these easy-to-follow recipes that take the stress out of entertaining and virtually guarantee success. From all-time classic dishes to modern flavors, there is a host of ideas that are sure to impress. If you are new to cooking, begin with the recipes in the Quick Meals and Easy Entertaining chapters as these recipes are the simplest to prepare. However, all of the recipes in this book are easy to follow, so don't be afraid to try something new.

The Newlyweds' Cookbook is comprehensive and inspiring. It will become an invaluable cooking partner during your new married life and many of the recipes are destined to become family favorites in the years ahead. It is a book that will make cooking for your loved one, family, and friends a true pleasure, whatever the occasion.

KITCHEN BASICS

*Before you even begin cooking, there is essential
equipment you will need to make your kitchen function
as it should. You will find this listed on page 11. It is also
a good idea to ensure your pantry is stocked with basic
cooking ingredients so you always have them to hand
when necessary. A well-stocked pantry will mean you can
put together a meal in minutes on those really hectic days
when you have no time to go shopping.*

utensils, pots, and pans

Whether you are a new cook or experienced in the kitchen, this list of essential equipment is what you will need to put the most basic of meals on the table. You may already have a number of these items, or received some of them as wedding gifts, so take all the equipment you already have out of the cupboards and drawers and lay it on the table. Check the list, opposite, to see if you have everything you need, then put it back in its place. If there's any equipment left on the table that you haven't used in the last 12 months, give it away. As funds allow, try to assemble all the equipment in the startup kit. Perhaps your friends and family can be persuaded to give you the items on the wish list for Christmas and birthdays.

Startup kit

For a basic set of equipment, buy the best you can afford, then it will last.

In your cupboards

1 nonstick skillet

1 nonstick wok with lid

1 heavy shallow pan with ovenproof handles for stovetop or oven cooking

3 saucepans—small, medium, and very large—with lids

1 collapsible metal steamer, bamboo steamer or 2-tier steaming saucepan

1 wire cooling rack

1 hand-held blender

1 sieve (strainer)

1 colander with legs or stand

1 box grater

1 set of mixing bowls

1 measuring cup

1 lemon juicer

1 salad spinner

On the shelf

1 kitchen scale

salt and pepper mills

1 coffee press and/or 1 teapot

In a block or wrap

1 paring or utility knife

1 large chopping knife

1 bread knife

1 pair of kitchen scissors

1 sharpening steel

On the work surface

1 heavy wooden chopping board

1 white heavy plastic board for raw meat and fish

1 roll of paper towels

In a large utensil pot

2 wooden spoons

1 large metal spoon

1 large slotted metal spoon

1 ladle

1 potato masher

1 long handled spatula

2 plastic spatulas

1 set of salad servers

1 pair of tongs

In the top drawer

1 potato peeler

1 can opener

1 corkscrew

2 metal skewers

1 rolling pin

In the bottom drawer

wax paper

aluminum foil

plastic wrap

medium freezer bags

large heavy-duty trash bags

1 roll of kitchen string

dishtowels

apron

oven mitts

For the oven

1 nonstick roasting pan

1 nonstick baking sheet

12-hole nonstick muffin pan

2 cake pans (8 inches diameter)

Wish list

Put these desirable objects on your "wish list" for Christmas and birthdays.

In your cupboards

1 food processor

1 electric mixer

1 blender

1 stovetop grill pan

6 ramekins (⅔ cup)

3 glass bowls—small, medium, and large

1 cooking thermometer

1 olive oil drizzler

1 mortar and pestle

In a large utensil pot

1 metal whisk

1 palette knife

1 meshed spoon for deep-frying

In the top drawer

baking parchment

large freezer bags

1 pastry brush

In the bottom drawer

more dishtowels (12 total)

another apron

another set of oven mitts

For the oven

another nonstick roasting pan

another nonstick baking sheet

1 loose-bottomed flan ring (10 inches diameter)

1 nonstick springform cake pan (8 inches diameter)

1 square cake pan

pantry essentials

It is a good idea to keep your pantry well stocked with useful ingredients that can be thrown together at a moment's notice to produce a quick meal. These are the essentials that are listed on the right. Fresh food should be bought often and in small quantities so it is always the freshest it can be. The food listed is just an illustration of the sorts of things you might want on hand at any one time.

Essentials

Staples

2–3 packages pasta, various shapes

2–3 packages rice—long grain, basmati, Thai fragrant, risotto

egg or rice noodles

dried lentils

all-purpose and self-rising flour

baking powder

coffee, tea, and sugar

Cans and cartons

vegetable broth

chicken broth

cans of: chopped tomatoes, chickpeas, cannellini and borlotti beans, anchovies in oil

coconut cream or milk

Oils and vinegars

large bottles of olive oil and peanut oil

small bottles of extra virgin olive oil for salads, peanut oil for frying, chile oil for flavoring

balsamic vinegar

Worcestershire sauce

red and white wine vinegar

Spices

whole nutmeg

ground cumin

ground coriander

ground turmeric

ground cinnamon and cinnamon sticks

sweet paprika

crushed dried chiles

Seasonings and flavorings

coarse sea salt

black peppercorns

soy sauce (light and dark)

Tabasco

teriyaki sauce

smooth Dijon mustard

honey

vanilla extract

Fresh food

a bag of onions

a head of garlic

red chiles

fresh ginger

fresh herbs, such as parsley

carrots

potatoes

tomatoes

lemons, limes, oranges, apples, and pears

In the refrigerator

eggs

milk

unsalted butter

a wedge of Parmesan cheese

feta cheese

plain yogurt

In the freezer

vanilla ice cream

frozen peas

ice cubes

Extra items

When you've got the basics, begin adding these extra ingredients for more adventurous cooking.

Staples

couscous or cracked wheat

bread flour

dry yeast

old-fashioned rolled oats

raisins

cocoa powder

white sugar

brown sugar

Oils and vinegars

small bottles of sesame oil and walnut oil

Spices

saffron threads

Seasonings and flavorings

Thai fish sauce

horseradish sauce

whole-grain mustard

English mustard powder

sun-dried tomatoes and peppers

black olives

capers

red wine

brandy

Marsala or sherry

Fresh food

your choice of other herbs, such as chives, basil, thyme, and rosemary

china, glassware, and flatware

Now that you are married, you may well be entertaining family and friends more frequently than you did previously. Even when just the two of you are eating together, it's important to make mealtimes special from time to time, especially at the end of a long week or when you are celebrating a special occasion. Using your best table- and glassware can make even the simplest food look and taste amazing. You may have received a number of the items listed on the opposite page as wedding gifts, or own them already, but here is a list of the necessary china, glassware, and tableware you will need to entertain a group of eight for dinner.

China

8 dinner plates

8 side plates

8 soup bowls

8 dessert plates or dishes

8 cups and saucers

Cutlery

8 dinner forks

8 salad forks

8 dinner knives

8 butter knives

8 steak knives

8 soup spoons

8 dessert spoons and/or forks

8 teaspoons

Serving pieces

2 ladles—1 large and 1 small

sugar spoon or tongs

salad servers

1 large, three-pronged fork

2–3 serving spoons

pie server

Serving dishes

2 platters—1 large
and 1 small

serving bowls—3 sizes

sauce or gravy boat

water pitcher

creamer

sugar bowl

teapot and/or coffee pot

small dishes, variety of

Glassware

8 water glasses

8 red wine glasses

8 white wine glasses

8 juice glasses

8 highball glasses

8 champagne flutes

8 brandy glasses

8 martini glasses

8 margarita glasses

8 liqueur glasses

Tableware

tablecloth

8 napkins

heatproof mats

BRUNCH

Breakfast during the week is often no more than a quick cup of coffee. The weekend offers a chance to enjoy a late start to the day with something delicious to eat. Preparing brunch for friends, your partner, or family need not mean a hectic start to the day for you. Get organized the night before and you can relax with your guests and really enjoy a long, leisurely brunch.

making the perfect cup of coffee

Coffee plants grow in sub-tropical climates around the world. Their fruit looks similar to cherries but over six to nine months will ripen to a very dark brown. Each "cherry" contains two coffee beans that are removed and then roasted; this caramelizes the sugars and carbohydrates in the bean and produces that distinctive flavor and aroma. How the beans are roasted will affect the flavor of the coffee. Dark roasted beans have a rather sharp, acidic flavor that is good for espresso, whereas lightly roasted beans have less caffeine and acidity and are best used in coffee presses or filters.

Blending and grinding

Blending is a complex art, but also a matter of taste. A specialist coffee merchant will make a blend to suit your personal taste—experiment with different brands and blends and beans from various parts of the world until you find your perfect cup.

The beans are ground according to the method you use to make your coffee: use coarsely ground coffee for a percolator, medium ground for a drip filter or coffee press and fine ground for espresso machines. For really good, fresh coffee, grind your own beans and keep the beans in an airtight container in the refrigerator. If you buy your coffee ready-ground, buy only what you need for the week and store it in the refrigerator.

Making coffee

As a rough guide, use 2 tablespoons of freshly ground coffee per cup if using a coffee press, drip filter, or espresso machine. Rinse the coffee press out with hot water, add the coffee, and fill with freshly boiled water. Let steep for 3 minutes, then gently push the plunger. Follow the manufacturer's directions for espresso machines. If you prefer white coffee, serve it with scalded milk for a real treat.

making the perfect cup of tea

Teas are classified according to the quality of the leaves; the younger the leaves, the better the tea. Broken larger leaves are used in lesser teas. Leaves are treated in different ways to make various teas:

Green tea is unfermented but roasted immediately after harvesting to give a clear infusion with a delicate taste.

Black tea is fermented and dried, giving an infusion with a strong taste and rich amber color. Varieties include Assam, Darjeeling, and Lapsang Souchong.

Oolong tea is a semi-fermented leaf that is fragrant with a sweet aftertaste.

Scented tea comes in many varieties, the most famous of which is Earl Grey, a black tea with oil of bergamot added. Other scented teas may have flowers, fruit, leaves, stems, or roots added.

Herbal teas or tisanes don't use real tea leaves. The many varieties include camomile and peppermint.

Making black, oolong, or scented tea

Always use freshly boiled filtered water. Rinse out the teapot with the boiled water, then add the tea, allowing 1 teaspoon per person and 1 for the pot. Pour in the boiled water and leave to infuse for 3 to 5 minutes. Do not over-infuse the tea or it will become bitter and dark. How strong and what to add, if anything, is a matter of personal taste. Tea can be drunk black, or with a dash of cold milk, with sugar, or a slice of lemon. Some people will only drink tea out of china mugs or cups—this is for you to choose.

Making green and herbal tea

These can be made in a mug for one person but if you are making tea for more than one, use a teapot. Green tea is best weak so calculate ½ teaspoon of tea per person, and the same for herbal. Many herbal teas come in individual bags and one of these per person is the best ratio. Brew for 1 minute—no longer or it will become bitter—then drink without milk or sugar.

This is so yummy—a gooey, sweet, fruity oatmeal made with a homemade granola mix, soaked overnight in cinnamon-infused milk. Add whatever berries or stone fruits take your fancy.

1¾ cups milk, plus extra to serve

½ teaspoon ground cinnamon

2 tablespoons honey

1½ cups fresh fruit and berries, such as strawberries, raspberries, and peaches

granola

2 cups rolled oats

½ cup oat bran

1 cup mixed nuts, such as hazelnuts, almonds, macadamias, and cashews, toasted and chopped

2 tablespoons sunflower seeds

2 tablespoons pumpkin seeds

2 tablespoons sesame seeds

⅓ cup raisins

⅔ cup mixed dried fruits, chopped, such as apricots, figs, dates, banana, and mango

serves 4

cinnamon-soaked granola *with fresh fruits*

To make the granola, put all the granola ingredients in a large bowl, mix well, and transfer to an airtight container. If you prefer toasted granola, put the oats in a skillet over medium heat and cook, stirring, until toasted and golden. Working in separate batches, repeat with the oat bran, nuts, and seeds. Let cool, then stir in the raisins and dried fruits. Store in an airtight container. You will need 4 cups granola, toasted or untoasted for this recipe, the remainder can be stored in the airtight container for up to 2 weeks.

Put the milk, cinnamon, and honey in a saucepan. Heat until almost boiling, then remove from the heat.

Divide 4 cups granola between 4 cereal bowls, pour over the hot milk, and let cool. Refrigerate overnight and serve at room temperature, topped with fresh fruit and berries of your choice and extra milk.

There isn't much to beat figs straight from the tree, bursting with sweetness and a sublime flavor.

fresh figs *with ricotta & honeycomb*

Arrange the figs and ricotta on a large plate and serve the honeycomb or honey in a separate bowl for everyone to help themselves.

1 lb. fresh ripe figs, about 8

1 lb. basket-formed ricotta cheese, sliced

a piece of honeycomb or ¼–½ cup honey

serves 4

Here is a classic brunch dish with a twist! If you don't have a waffle iron, simply drop a ladle of batter onto a lightly greased, heated skillet and sauté on both sides until golden.

waffles *with maple syrup ice cream*

ice cream

2 cups heavy cream

1 cup milk

seeds from 1 vanilla bean

5 egg yolks (to separate eggs, see page 147)

½ cup maple syrup, plus extra to serve

waffles

1 cup all-purpose flour

1 teaspoon baking powder

½ teaspoon baking soda

1 tablespoon sugar

½ cup buttermilk

1 egg, lightly beaten

6 tablespoons butter, melted

an ice cream maker (optional)

a waffle iron, lightly greased

serves 6

To make the ice cream, put the cream, milk, and vanilla seeds in a saucepan and heat until the mixture reaches boiling point. Remove from the heat and set aside.

Meanwhile, put the egg yolks and syrup in a bowl and beat to mix. Stir in the heated cream mixture and return to the pan. Heat gently, stirring, until the mixture thickens enough to coat the back of a wooden spoon. Do not let the mixture boil or it will curdle. Remove from the heat and let cool.

Freeze in an ice cream maker, following the manufacturer's instructions. If you don't have an ice cream maker, pour the mixture into flat freezer trays and put them in the freezer. Let the mixture partially freeze, beat to break up the ice crystals, and return the trays to the freezer. Repeat several times—the more you do it, the smoother the end result.

To make the waffles, sift the flour, baking powder, and baking soda into a bowl. Stir in the sugar. In a second bowl, beat the buttermilk, egg, and butter together, then add to the dry ingredients and beat until smooth. Spoon a layer of the batter into a heated waffle iron and spread flat. Cook for about 1 minute until crisp and golden. Serve hot with a scoop of ice cream and a little extra maple syrup poured over. Repeat with the remaining waffle batter.

1½ cups all-purpose flour

2 teaspoons baking powder

1 teaspoon salt

3 tablespoons sugar

1 cup milk

2 eggs, lightly beaten

4 tablespoons unsalted butter, melted, plus extra for cooking

maple butter syrup

⅓ cup maple syrup

2 tablespoons unsalted butter

a cast-iron skillet or flat-surfaced griddle

makes 8–12, serves 4

pancakes

Sift the flour, baking powder, salt, and sugar into a bowl. Mix the milk, eggs, and the melted butter in a large pitcher, then add the flour mixture and mix quickly to make a batter (don't worry about lumps—they're good). Alternatively, make the batter in a bowl and transfer to a pitcher.

Heat a cast-iron skillet or flat-surfaced griddle until medium hot, grease lightly with extra butter, and pour in the batter in batches to make rounds, 3 to 4 inches in diameter. Cook for 1 to 2 minutes or until bubbles form on top of the pancakes and the undersides are golden, then flip the pancakes over and cook for 1 minute. Keep them warm in the oven while you cook the remaining batches.

To make the maple butter syrup, heat the maple syrup and butter together in a small saucepan or microwave until the butter has melted. Stack the pancakes on warmed plates and pour over the buttery syrup. Serve immediately.

bitter chocolate & orange muffins

Nothing beats a home-baked muffin with a cup of steaming coffee or tea for a special treat.

1¾ cups plus 1 tablespoon all-purpose flour
1½ teaspoons baking powder
1 teaspoon salt
½ teaspoon baking soda
1⅛ cups sugar
3 oz. bitter chocolate (at least 70 percent cocoa solids), coarsely chopped
grated zest and juice of 1 unwaxed orange
4 tablespoons butter
¾ cup milk

a 12-cup muffin pan, lightly greased

makes 12 muffins

Sift the flour, baking powder, salt, and baking soda into a large bowl. Stir in the sugar, chopped chocolate, and orange zest and make a well in the center of the dry ingredients.

Put the butter in a small saucepan and heat until melted. Remove the pan from the heat, then stir in the milk and orange juice. Pour the butter and orange mixture into the well of the dry ingredients and stir briefly with a wooden spoon. Do not overmix—the batter should be lumpy, not smooth. Spoon the batter into the prepared pan, filling each cup three-quarters full.

Bake in a preheated oven at 375°F for about 20 minutes until golden and cooked through. (Insert a skewer into the center of one muffin to test—the skewer should come out clean.)

Remove the muffins from the oven and let cool in the pan for a couple of minutes, then invert onto a wire rack to cool slightly. Serve warm or at room temperature.

blueberry muffins

Though they're best eaten hot from the oven, these muffins can be made the night before, left to cool, stored in an airtight container, then reheated before serving.

2 cups all-purpose flour
1 teaspoon baking powder
¼ teaspoon salt
1 cup sugar
2 eggs, lightly beaten
6 tablespoons butter, melted, or sunflower oil
1 teaspoon pure vanilla extract
½ cup low-fat plain yogurt
1½ cups blueberries

a large 6-cup or small 12-cup muffin pan, lightly greased

makes 6 large or 12 small muffins

Sift the flour and baking powder into a bowl and stir in the salt Add the remaining ingredients and fold everything together until just blended; do not beat or overmix. Spoon the batter into the prepared pan, filling each cup three-quarters full.

Bake in a preheated oven at 350°F for 20 to 30 minutes, until golden and firm to the touch. (Insert a skewer into the center of one muffin to test—the skewer should come out clean.) Remove the muffins from the oven and let cool in the pan for a couple of minutes, then invert onto a wire rack to cool slightly. Serve warm or at room temperature.

Greasing, flouring, and lining baking pans

• *"Greasing" means brushing the inside of the pan with a thin film of butter or oil. This stops the food from sticking to the pan when cooked.*

• *Also to stop the food sticking, pans are sometimes then dusted with a light layer of flour, or lined with parchment paper on the base, or on the base and sides.*

• *Lining is usually done if the food is to be baked for a long time, such as a large fruitcake.*

Charring the asparagus spears on a stovetop grill pan intensifies their flavor and adds a smokiness to the frittata.

charred asparagus & herb frittata
with smoked salmon

8 oz. asparagus spears

1 tablespoon extra virgin olive oil

6 eggs

4 scallions, finely chopped

2 tablespoons chopped fresh herbs, such as tarragon, dill, and mint

¼ cup fresh ricotta cheese

1 tablespoon butter

sea salt and cracked black pepper

to serve

8 oz. smoked salmon

sour cream or crème fraîche

lemon wedges

a stovetop grill pan

serves 4

Trim the asparagus and toss with the oil and a little salt and pepper. Heat a stovetop grill pan until hot, add the asparagus, and cook for 3 to 4 minutes, turning until evenly charred. Set aside to cool.

Put the eggs in a bowl and beat until evenly mixed. Stir in the scallions, herbs, ricotta, and salt and pepper to taste.

Melt the butter in a large nonstick skillet, add the egg mixture, and swirl to the edge of the pan. Arrange the asparagus spears over the top and cook for 3 to 4 minutes until the eggs are set underneath.

Put the pan briefly under a hot broiler to cook the top of the frittata, then remove from the heat and let cool to room temperature.

Cut the frittata into slices and serve with the smoked salmon, sour cream or crème fraîche, and lemon wedges.

creamy eggs *with arugula pesto*

Creamy scrambled eggs topped with arugula pesto are especially good on top of a crunchy nut bread.

To make the arugula pesto, chop the arugula coarsely, then transfer to a food processor. Add the basil, almonds, oil, garlic, salt, and pepper, and purée briefly to form a vivid green paste. Transfer to a bowl and stir in the cheese. Set aside.

Put the eggs and cream in a bowl, beat with a fork, then add salt and pepper, to taste. Put the butter in a large nonstick saucepan, melt gently, then add the egg mixture and cook over low heat, stirring with a wooden spoon, until the eggs have just set.

Put a slice of toast onto each plate, top with the scrambled eggs, and serve immediately, with a spoonful of arugula pesto.

12 eggs

¼ cup heavy cream

4 tablespoons butter

6 slices nut or seeded bread, toasted

sea salt and freshly ground black pepper

arugula pesto

2 oz. arugula

2 tablespoons chopped fresh basil leaves

2 tablespoons blanched almonds, chopped

⅓ cup extra virgin olive oil

1 garlic clove, chopped

2 tablespoons freshly grated pecorino or Parmesan cheese

serves 6

Smoked salmon and baked eggs make the perfect breakfast treat—
it's an easy, elegant dish that takes no time at all.

baked eggs
with smoked salmon & chives

8 oz. smoked salmon slices, chopped

1 tablespoon chopped fresh chives

4 eggs

¼ cup heavy cream

freshly ground black pepper

toast, to serve

4 ramekins or shallow dishes,
1 cup each, well buttered

serves 4

Divide the smoked salmon and chives between the 4 buttered ramekins. Make a small indent in the salmon with the back of a spoon and break an egg into the hollow. Sprinkle with a little pepper and spoon the cream over the top.

Put the ramekins in a roasting pan and half-fill the pan with boiling water. Bake in a preheated oven at 350°F for 10 to 15 minutes until the eggs have just set. Remove from the oven, let cool for a few minutes, then serve with toast.

Try substituting smoked salmon for the ham or, for
vegetarians, replace the ham with wilted spinach.

eggs benedict

4 large slices of prosciutto or country ham

1 tablespoon vinegar

4 eggs

4 English muffins

sea salt and cracked black pepper

hollandaise sauce

3 egg yolks (to separate eggs, see page 147)

2 tablespoons water

1 teaspoon freshly squeezed lemon juice

2 sticks unsalted butter, melted

serves 4

To make the hollandaise sauce, put the egg yolks, water, and lemon juice in a blender and process until frothy. With the motor running, gradually pour in the melted butter in a steady stream until the sauce is thickened and glossy. Transfer the sauce to a heatproof bowl set over a saucepan of hot water. Cover and keep the sauce warm.

Broil or sauté the slices of prosciutto until really crisp and keep them warm in a low oven. To poach the eggs, bring a saucepan of lightly salted water to a boil. Add the vinegar and reduce to the heat so the water simmers gently. Swirl the water well with a fork and crack 2 eggs into the water. Cook for 3 minutes, then remove with a slotted spoon. Repeat with the remaining 2 eggs.

Meanwhile, toast the muffins whole. Top each one with a slice of crisp prosciutto, then a poached egg. Spoon over the hollandaise sauce, sprinkle with salt and pepper, and serve at once.

This is a good substantial brunch dish and makes great comfort food. Roasting the tomatoes really brings out their juicy flavors and they make the perfect partner for the crispy potatoes.

hash browns *with sausages & oven roasted tomatoes*

Cook the potatoes in a large saucepan of lightly salted, boiling water for 10 to 12 minutes, until almost cooked through. Drain well and mash coarsely.

Melt the butter in a large nonstick skillet, add the onion, and sauté gently for 15 minutes until soft and golden. Add the potatoes to the pan with salt and pepper, to taste. Cook, stirring and mashing the potatoes occasionally, for 15 to 20 minutes until well-browned and crisp around the edges.

Meanwhile, put the sausages in a roasting pan, drizzle with half the oil, and roast on the middle shelf of a preheated oven at 400°F for 25 minutes.

Put the tomatoes, still on the vine, in a shallow ovenproof dish. Drizzle with the remaining oil and put on the top shelf of the oven after the sausages have been cooking for 5 minutes. Cook the tomatoes for 15 minutes, then drizzle over the balsamic vinegar and cook for 5 minutes more.

Spoon the hash browns onto warmed plates and top with the sausages, tomatoes, and their juice. Serve immediately.

1½ lb. baking potatoes, such as russets, peeled and diced

4 tablespoons butter

1 large onion, finely chopped

12 good-quality breakfast sausages

2 tablespoons olive oil

2 cups cherry tomatoes

1 tablespoon balsamic vinegar

sea salt and freshly ground black pepper

serves 4

mushrooms on toast
with melted cheese

Large, juicy mushrooms need little embellishment—just a slice of cheese and a hint of sweetness from the brioche.

Melt the butter in a skillet, add the mushrooms, and cook for 8 to 10 minutes, until golden and beginning to give up their juices. Add salt and pepper to taste.

Meanwhile, toast the brioche or bread slices on both sides under a preheated broiler. Spoon over the mushrooms and their juices and top with the Taleggio slices. Return the topped brioche to the broiler for a few seconds, so that the cheese just begins to melt. Serve at once.

½ cup butter

8 portobello mushrooms, wiped and trimmed

4 slices of brioche or whole-wheat bread

4 oz. Taleggio or other rich semi-soft cheese, sliced

sea salt and freshly ground black pepper

serves 4

kick-starter bloody mary

crushed ice
5 lemons
I cup vodka
3 inches white horseradish, freshly grated, or I tablespoon bottled horseradish
I tablespoon Worcestershire sauce
I teaspoon Tabasco sauce
3 cups tomato juice, well chilled
freshly ground black pepper
celery stalks, with leaves, to serve

serves 4

If you or your guests can't face alcohol so early in the day, make one pitcher of this and one pitcher of Virgin Mary (see page 175), which is made without the vodka.

Half-fill a large pitcher with crushed ice. Cut I lemon into slices and squeeze the juice from the others. Add the lemons and the juice to the pitcher, together with all the other ingredients except the celery. Mix well. Serve in 4 highball glasses with a celery stalk.

tropical smoothie

I ripe mango
I ripe banana, coarsely chopped
grated zest and juice of I unwaxed lime
⅓ cup freshly squeezed orange juice

serves 2

Use a juicy, ripe mango to make this smoothie—it should be really fragrant.

To slice the mango, cut off both sides of the fruit either side of the seed. Peel back the skin and, at the same time, scoop out the flesh with a spoon. Cut the flesh into slices. Peel off the remaining skin from the mango and, using a knife, cut as much flesh as you can from the seed. Put the mango slices, bananas, lime zest and juice, and orange juice in a blender or food processor and process until smooth. Pour into 2 glasses and serve at once.

very berry smoothie

I cup strawberries, hulled
I cup raspberries
½ cup blueberries
¾ cup cranberry juice
¼ cup plain yogurt
I teaspoon honey
4 large ice cubes

serves 2

The plain yogurt in this bright, summery smoothie adds a creamy taste and color to the red berries. Add more or less honey, depending on your taste.

Put 2 tall glasses in the freezer to chill.

Put all the ingredients in a blender or food processor and process until almost smooth. Taste for sweetness, adding more honey, if needed. Pour into the 2 chilled glasses and serve immediately.

SNACKS, APPETIZERS, & SALADS

These little dishes can be served at any time of the day. They are perfect for lunch, whether you are looking for a quick snack or a more leisurely meal to be enjoyed with family and friends. Many can be used as an appetizer, or as a snack when you get home late and need something satisfying to eat, as well as something quick and easy to prepare.

pan-grilled bruschetta
with onion marmalade & goat cheese

2 ciabatta rolls, cut in half crosswise

4 large handfuls of mixed salad leaves

1 tablespoon extra virgin olive oil, plus extra for serving

¼ cup Red Onion Marmalade (see page 181)

½ cup soft, mild goat cheese

sea salt and freshly ground black pepper

a stovetop grill pan

serves 4

Char-grilled bread is more than just toast—it stays chewy on the inside, has a smoky flavor, and lovely stripes from the grill pan.

Heat a stovetop grill pan until hot. Add the ciabatta and cook for 1 to 2 minutes on each side until lightly toasted and charred.

Meanwhile, put the salad leaves in a bowl, then add the olive oil and salt and pepper to taste. Toss well.

Spread the onion marmalade on the toasted ciabatta and put onto serving plates. Top with a handful of salad leaves and crumble the goat cheese over the salad. Sprinkle with olive oil and lots of black pepper and serve.

This is such a classic sandwich and really very delicious. Always use the freshest bread for this snack and choose a nice crusty loaf, if you can.

steak & tomato sandwich

olive oil, for greasing

4 small sirloin steaks, 3 oz. each

8 slices of bread

butter, for spreading

4 teaspoons Dijon mustard

2 large, ripe tomatoes, sliced

4 oz. arugula

sea salt and freshly ground black pepper

a stovetop grill pan (optional)

serves 4

Brush a stovetop grill pan or a nonstick skillet with a little olive oil and heat until hot. Add the steaks to the pan and cook for 1 minute on each side for rare steak, 2 minutes each side for medium, or 3 minutes each side for well done.

Spread 4 slices of the bread with butter and mustard, then add the sliced tomatoes and arugula.

Top with the cooked steak and sprinkle with salt and pepper. Butter the remaining slices of bread and put them on top of the steaks. Press together and serve.

1 lb. boneless pork shoulder (fat not trimmed), ground

1 lb. veal, ground

8 oz. calves' liver, finely chopped

1 egg, beaten

2 shallots, finely chopped

2 garlic cloves, crushed

1 tablespoon coarse sea salt

2 tablespoons green peppercorns in brine, drained, plus extra for decorating

½ teaspoon ground allspice

3 tablespoons Cognac

a handful of fresh bay leaves (see method)

freshly ground black pepper

to serve

French cornichons

sliced baguette

unsalted butter

a rectangular terrine mold, 12 x 4 inches

parchment paper

serves 10-12

This terrine is simplicity itself. If you ask your butcher to grind all the meat, except the liver, then it will be even easier. Serve in slices to begin an informal meal, with plenty of fresh baguette, unsalted butter, and French cornichons.

rustic pâté *with green peppercorns*

Put the pork, veal, and liver in a large bowl. Add the egg, shallots, garlic, salt, pepper, green peppercorns, allspice, and Cognac and mix well, preferably with your hands.

Fill the mold with the meat mixture, patting to spread evenly. Arrange bay leaves on top of the mold and dot with extra green peppercorns. Set the mold in a roasting pan and add enough boiling water to come halfway up the sides of the mold. Cover the terrine with foil and bake in a preheated oven at 350°F until a knife inserted in the middle is hot to the touch after 30 seconds, about 1½ hours.

Remove from the oven and let cool. When the pâté is at room temperature, cover with parchment paper and weight with a few food cans. Refrigerate, with the weights on top, for at least 1 day, but ideally for 3 days. The pâté will keep, refrigerated, for 1 week. Bring to room temperature before serving with French cornichons, slices of baguette, and butter.

warm chunky salmon pâté

This shouldn't be a smooth pâté, so flake the cooked fish into big pieces.

Put the salmon, skin side up, in a shallow microwave dish. Add the wine and cover with microwave-safe plastic wrap. Cook on MEDIUM for 5 minutes.

Meanwhile, put the cream cheese, yogurt, dill, and lemon juice in a large bowl and mix well.

Drain the fish on paper towels and flake into large pieces. Gently fold the fish into the cream cheese mixture and season to taste with salt and pepper. Serve the pâté with toast and lemon wedges.

6 oz. salmon fillet, skin on

⅔ cup white wine

½ cup cream cheese

¼ cup plain yogurt

2 tablespoons coarsely chopped fresh dill

a squeeze of fresh lemon juice

sea salt and freshly ground black pepper

to serve

pumpernickel or rye bread, toasted

1 lemon, cut into wedges

serves 4

eggplant antipasto *with pine nuts & herbs*

2–3 medium eggplants, about 1½ lb.

2 tablespoons sea salt flakes

½ cup extra virgin olive oil

½ cup pine nuts

1 small bunch of fresh mint, half chopped, half in sprigs

1 small bunch of fresh flat-leaf parsley, half chopped, half in sprigs

2 tablespoons aged balsamic vinegar

freshly ground black pepper

a stovetop grill pan

serves 4-6

A simple, delicious snack or appetizer, with mellow olive oil accentuating the flavors.

Slice the eggplants lengthwise into ½-inch slices. Score both sides of each slice with a fork. Sprinkle with salt. Let drain on a rack for 20 minutes, then pat dry with paper towels.

Heat a ridged stovetop grill pan until very hot. Wipe the pan with olive oil using a wad of crumpled paper towel or a heatproof brush. Brush each slice of eggplant with olive oil. Press the eggplant down firmly on the hot pan and cook for 3 to 5 minutes on each side, in batches if necessary, until grill-marked, tender, and aromatic. Heat 1 tablespoon olive oil in a skillet, add the pine nuts, and toast gently until golden. Remove from the pan and set aside.

Sprinkle the cooked eggplant with chopped mint, chopped parsley, pepper, and a few drops of balsamic vinegar. Loop the slices on serving plates, add the pine nuts and sprigs of mint and parsley, and serve.

spanish potato omelet

Heat the oil in a medium skillet, add the potatoes and onion, and cook over low heat for 12 to 14 minutes or until tender but not browned, moving them about with a spatula so that they cook evenly. Add the garlic, if using, for the last 2 minutes.

Put the eggs, salt, and pepper in a bowl and beat well. Using a slotted spoon, remove the cooked potatoes and garlic from the pan and stir it into the egg mixture. Stir in the chopped parsley or scallion tops. Quickly pour the egg mixture back into the hot skillet. Cook, not stirring, over low to moderate heat for 4 to 5 minutes or until firm, but do not let it brown too much. The top will still be wobbly, only part-cooked.

Holding a heatproof plate over the top of the omelet, quickly invert the pan, omelet, and plate. Slide the hot omelet upside down, back into the pan to brown the other side for 2 to 3 minutes more. Remove from the pan and let cool for 5 minutes.

To make the sauce, put the sweet peppers, ⅓ cup of the liquid from the can (make it up with water if necessary), and the sherry vinegar in a blender. Purée to form a smooth, scarlet sauce. Cut the omelet into chunks, wedges, or cubes. Serve the sauce separately, spooning some over the omelet.

½ cup extra virgin olive oil

2 lb. boiling potatoes, peeled and cut into 1-inch cubes

1 onion, sliced into rings

4 garlic cloves, finely chopped (optional)

6 eggs, beaten

¼ cup chopped fresh flat-leaf parsley or scallion tops

sea salt and freshly ground black pepper

piquillo sauce

8 oz. can or jar of roasted sweet peppers, such as piquillos or pimientos

3 tablespoons sherry vinegar

serves 4-6

This classic French soup is ideal when it's chilly outside and people are hungry inside.

french onion soup

3 tablespoons unsalted butter

1 tablespoon extra virgin olive oil

3 large onions, about 3 lb., thinly sliced

2 garlic cloves, crushed

1 tablespoon all-purpose flour

1 quart beef or chicken broth

2¾ cups dry white wine

1 fresh bay leaf

2 sprigs of thyme

1 baguette, or other white bread, sliced

1½ cups freshly grated Gruyère cheese, about 5 oz.

coarse sea salt and freshly ground black pepper

a baking sheet

serves 4-6

Put the butter and oil in a large saucepan and melt over medium heat. Add the onions and cook over low heat until soft, 15 to 20 minutes.

Add the garlic and flour and cook, stirring, for about 1 minute. Add the broth, wine, bay leaf, and thyme. Season with salt and pepper and bring to a boil. Boil for 1 minute, then lower the heat and simmer very gently for 20 minutes. Taste and adjust the seasoning with salt and pepper, if necessary. At this point, the soup will be cooked, but standing time will improve the flavor—at least 30 minutes.

Before serving, preheat the broiler. Put the baguette slices on a baking sheet and brown under the broiler until lightly toasted. Set aside.

To serve, reheat the soup, then ladle it into ovenproof bowls. Top with a few toasted baguette slices, sprinkle grated cheese over the top, and cook under the hot broiler until the cheese is browned and bubbling. Serve immediately.

butternut squash soup

The key to this soup is the light spicing and the roasting of the butternut squash to bring out its sweet flavor.

Put the butternut squash halves flesh side down on the baking sheet. Roast in a preheated oven at 375°F for 45 minutes or until tender. Remove from the oven and, using a spoon, scoop the flesh out of the skins into a bowl. Discard the skins.

Put the butter in a large saucepan and melt over medium to low heat. Add the leek, bay leaf, peppercorns, and allspice and sauté gently until the leek begins to soften. Add the butternut squash, broth, and 1 quart water. Bring to a boil, reduce the heat, and simmer for about 10 minutes, or until the leeks are very soft.

Remove the bay leaf and transfer the soup to a blender. Add the pine nuts and blend until smooth, working in batches if necessary. Return the soup to the saucepan and reheat. Serve hot with crusty bread.

1 butternut squash, cut in half lengthwise and seeded

2 tablespoons unsalted butter

1 large leek, trimmed and chopped

1 fresh bay leaf

a few black peppercorns, crushed

4–5 allspice berries, crushed

2¾ cups Vegetable Broth (see page 178)

¾ cup pine nuts, toasted in a dry skillet

crusty bread, to serve

a nonstick baking sheet

serves 4

1½ lb. vine-ripened tomatoes

1 large shallot, or 1 small red onion, thinly sliced

coarse sea salt and freshly ground black pepper

anchovy vinaigrette

1 garlic clove

½ teaspoon Dijon mustard

2 tablespoons white wine vinegar

6 anchovy fillets, packed in oil

½ cup extra virgin olive oil

a small handful of fresh basil leaves

to serve

a handful of fresh flat-leaf parsley, finely chopped

a few fresh basil leaves, torn

serves 4

"Anchoïade" is a Provençal anchovy sauce/dip that is spread thickly on grilled bread slices, or served with raw vegetables as an appetizer. Here it is used as a dressing for what will hopefully be very ripe, flavorful tomatoes. If these are not available, use boiled baby new potatoes.

tomato salad *with anchovy vinaigrette*

To make the vinaigrette, put the garlic, mustard, vinegar, and anchovies in a small food processor and blend well. Add the oil, 1 tablespoon at a time, then blend in the basil. Season with pepper and set aside.

Cut the tomatoes into quarters or eighths, depending on their size. Arrange them on a plate and sprinkle with the shallot. Season lightly with salt, then spoon the vinaigrette over the top. Sprinkle with the parsley, basil, and some black pepper, and serve at room temperature.

2 red bell peppers, cut in half and seeded

2 yellow bell peppers, cut in half and seeded

1 lb. ripe plum tomatoes, about 4 medium

¼ cup red wine vinegar

2 garlic cloves, crushed to a paste with coarse sea salt

½ cup extra virgin olive oil, plus extra for drizzling

2 tablespoons capers

⅓ cup black olives, pitted

1 small or ½ large loaf day-old ciabatta, cut coarsely into cubes

a bunch of fresh basil, leaves torn

freshly ground black pepper

a baking sheet

serves 4–6

tuscan panzanella

The bread will drink up the rich flavors of the dressing, so use a crusty, firm-crumbed bread, such as ciabatta.

Put the peppers cut side down on a baking sheet and broil under a preheated broiler until blistered and charred. Transfer to a plastic bag, seal, and let cool (the steam will loosen the skin, making it easier to peel). Scrape off the skin, then cut the peppers into strips, reserving any juice.

Cut the tomatoes in half and scoop out the cores and seeds over a bowl to catch the juice. Purée the cores and seeds in a blender, then press the extra juice through a strainer into the bowl. Discard the pulp and seeds. Cut the tomato halves into strips.

Put the tomato juice, vinegar, garlic, and black pepper in a bowl. Gradually add the olive oil, whisking until blended.

Put the strips of pepper and tomato in a bowl, add the capers, olives, ciabatta, and basil and mix. Add the tomato dressing, toss well to coat, then set aside for 1 hour to develop the flavors. Drizzle with extra olive oil and serve.

This shouldn't be made too far in advance, or the salad will go soggy and the avocado will discolor.

bacon, avocado, & feta salad

16 slices of bacon

10 oz. package mixed salad leaves

3 ripe avocados, sliced

4 ripe tomatoes, cut into wedges

8 oz. feta cheese, about 2 oz. per person

a large handful of fresh flat-leaf parsley, coarsely chopped

a large handful of fresh cilantro, coarsely chopped

freshly ground black pepper

dressing

¼ cup wine vinegar

½ teaspoon fine sea salt

1½ teaspoons Dijon mustard

about ¾ cup extra virgin olive oil

serves 4

Cook the bacon in a hot nonstick skillet until crisp. Transfer to a plate lined with paper towels and set aside.

To make the dressing, put the vinegar and salt in a small bowl. Using a small whisk or fork, stir until the salt dissolves. Beat in the mustard, then gradually beat in the oil, 1 tablespoon at a time. Taste when you've added 12 tablespoons. If it's too sharp, add a few more tablespoons, beating well.

Put the salad leaves in a large bowl and add about 6 tablespoons of the dressing—the leaves should be just coated, not drowning. Toss well, then divide the leaves between 4 plates.

Cut each slice of bacon into 3 to 4 pieces and share between the plates, on top of the leaves (about 4 slices per plate). Arrange equal amounts of avocado and tomato on each plate. Divide the feta into 4 portions and crumble it over each serving. Sprinkle with the parsley and cilantro. Trickle the remaining dressing over the top and finish with a generous grinding of black pepper. Serve.

peppered goat cheese

1 tablespoon freshly ground black pepper

2 goat cheeses, 4 oz. each, with rind, cut in half crosswise

2 large handfuls of arugula

2 large handfuls of baby leaf spinach

1 tablespoon extra virgin olive oil

freshly squeezed juice of ½ lemon

sea salt

Chile Oil, to serve (optional, see page 181)

a stovetop grill pan

serves 4

Cheeses, especially blue, goat milk, or creamy ones, make excellent salads. Gentle cooking gives this one extra pizzazz.

Sprinkle the pepper onto a plate. Lightly press both sides of each cheese slice into the pepper to coat.

Heat a stovetop grill pan until hot. Add the peppered cheese slices, cut side down, and cook for 2 minutes. Turn them over, cover loosely with foil, and cook for a further 4 to 5 minutes until the cheese is soft but not melted.

Put the arugula, spinach, oil, and lemon juice in a large bowl. Add salt to taste and toss to coat. Divide the salad between 4 large serving plates or flat bowls and top with a slice of grilled cheese. Sprinkle with chile oil, if using, and serve.

italian mixed salad

If you ask for a mixed salad in Italy, this is what you will get. Oil and vinegar are served at the table so you can dress the salad yourself.

12 oz. new potatoes, peeled
6 oz. fine green beans, trimmed
about 1 tablespoon extra virgin olive oil
¼ cup black or green olives, pitted
1 small crisp lettuce
2 large ripe tomatoes, quartered (or unripe to be authentic)
3 tablespoons chopped fresh parsley
sea salt and freshly ground black pepper

to serve
a small bottle of good olive oil
a small bottle of red wine vinegar

serves 4

Boil the potatoes in a saucepan of lightly salted boiling water for about 15 minutes or until tender, adding the beans 4 minutes before the potatoes are ready. Drain and cover with cold water to stop the vegetables cooking.

When cold, drain well. Remove the beans to a bowl, slice the potatoes thickly, and add to the beans, moistening with a little olive oil. Add the olives and toss well.

Wash the lettuce and tear into bite-size pieces. Add the lettuce and tomatoes to the potatoes and beans and toss lightly. Transfer to a serving bowl and sprinkle with parsley, salt, and pepper. Serve the olive oil and vinegar separately and dress the salad at the table.

Washing and drying salad leaves

- *Wash crisp-leaved lettuces and other salad leaves in a bowl of water, transfer to a salad spinner, and spin dry. Wrap in a cloth or paper towels and store in the refrigerator—the leaves will become even crisper.*
- *Rinse soft-leaved greens, such as mâche or arugula just before using and let drain in a colander. Pat dry with paper towels and serve as soon as possible.*

---

salade niçoise

This classic French salad is extremely versatile—it is delicious served as a lunch, an appetizer, or even as a one-dish supper.

14 oz. fresh tuna steak, cut into 4 pieces
4 medium new potatoes, cooked and sliced
4 tomatoes, peeled* and cut into wedges
4 oz. green beans, trimmed, halved, and cooked
1 red onion, sliced
4 baby romaine lettuce, quartered lengthwise
4 hard-cooked eggs, peeled and cut in half
4 anchovies, cut into long strips
12 black olives, pitted
a bunch of flat-leaf parsley, coarsely chopped
¼ cup olive oil
¼ cup balsamic vinegar
sea salt and freshly ground black pepper
1 lemon, cut into wedges, to serve

a stovetop grill pan (optional)

serves 4

Heat a stovetop grill pan or broiler, add the tuna, and cook for 1 to 2 minutes on each side. Remove from the heat, set aside, and keep it warm.

Put the cooked sliced potatoes in a bowl with the tomato wedges, beans, onion, lettuce, and eggs. Add the anchovies, olives, parsley, olive oil, balsamic vinegar, salt, and pepper, to taste. Mix carefully.

Serve the salad topped with the tuna and accompanied by wedges of lemon. Alternatively, the traditional way to serve this salad is to arrange groups of the ingredients on a large platter, drizzle with the olive oil and vinegar, then serve.

*Note To peel tomatoes, bring a saucepan of water to a boil, cut a cross in the skin at the base of each tomato, then plunge them into the boiling water for 20 seconds. Drain, then peel the skin away when the tomatoes are cool enough to handle.

QUICK MEALS

It is wonderful to spend time cooking long, leisurely meals, but in reality, at the end of a busy day many of us don't have that luxury. If you and your partner work hard during the week, you will want food that is quick to prepare and on the table in minutes. These recipes provide all the inspiration you need to create fast, simple, delicious dishes when time is short. They are much better for you than a takeout and ready in the same amount of time.

16 oz. pasta, dried, fresh, or stuffed, freshly cooked

3 tablespoons freshly grated Parmesan cheese, plus extra to serve

a handful of fresh herbs, torn or finely chopped (optional)

tomato sauce

2 cans plum tomatoes, about 14 oz. each, drained (reserve the juice), seeded, and chopped

⅓ cup extra virgin olive oil, plus extra to serve

4 garlic cloves

your choice of:
I small piece of fresh chile, ½ cinnamon stick, ½ teaspoon dried oregano, or a bunch of fresh herbs such as basil

sea salt and freshly ground black pepper

serves 4-6

This classic pasta sauce is made simply with tomatoes, olive oil, garlic, and the flavoring of your choice. The use of canned plum tomatoes make this a handy pantry standby.

quick neapolitan tomato sauce

To make the tomato sauce, put the prepared tomatoes, oil, and garlic in a heavy saucepan. Add your choice of the chile, cinnamon, and dried or fresh herbs. Cover and simmer over low heat for 30 minutes, or until the tomatoes are reduced to a creamy mass. Stir from time to time to stop the sauce sticking to the bottom of the pan. Add a little of the reserved tomato juice when necessary to keep the sauce moist.

Discard the garlic and chile, cinnamon, or any woody herb stems and mash the sauce with a potato masher. If you prefer a smooth sauce, pass it through a blender. Season to taste with salt and freshly ground black pepper.

Pour the sauce over the freshly cooked pasta, top with the Parmesan, and stir well. Transfer to a serving dish, sprinkle with fresh herbs, if using, then serve at once with extra Parmesan and a drizzle of olive oil.

penne *with mozzarella*

Bring a large saucepan of water to a boil, then add a large pinch of salt. Add the penne and cook until al dente, about 8 minutes.

Meanwhile, to make the sauce, put the tomatoes in a large, shallow saucepan or skillet. Add the chile, garlic, onion, tomato paste, oregano, sugar, balsamic vinegar, if using, and capers or olives. Cook, stirring, over high heat until the sauce is thick and reduced to half its original volume. Add salt and pepper to taste.

Drain the pasta, reserving 3 tablespoons of the cooking liquid, then return the pasta and reserved liquid to the saucepan. Add the sliced mozzarella. Pour the hot sauce over the top and toss and stir until well mixed and the mozzarella is soft and melting. Sprinkle with the olive oil and serve topped with sprigs of basil.

Variation This dish can also be made in advance. Cook the pasta and make the sauce as in the main recipe. Pour both into a heatproof baking dish, but do not add the cheese. When ready to cook, bake in a preheated oven at 350°F for 25 to 35 minutes or until very hot, bubbling, and fragrant. Add the cheese and drizzle the oil on top. Bake for 2 minutes more until the cheese melts, then serve.

14 oz. penne rigate

14 oz. canned chopped plum tomatoes

I small dried red chile

3–4 garlic cloves, chopped

I onion, chopped

2 tablespoons tomato paste

leaves from 2 sprigs of oregano or basil, chopped or torn

I tablespoon sugar

I tablespoon balsamic vinegar (optional)

2 tablespoons capers, or black olives, rinsed and drained (optional)

sea salt and freshly ground black pepper

to serve

6 oz. mozzarella cheese, thinly sliced

2 tablespoons extra virgin olive oil

sprigs of basil

serves 4

greek omelet

1 cup cherry tomatoes, cut in half

4–5 pickled golden hot Greek peppers, drained and sliced

3 scallions, sliced

⅓ cup pitted black olives, sliced

4 oz. feta cheese

a small handful of flat-leaf parsley, chopped

6 extra-large eggs

fine sea salt and freshly ground black pepper

crusty bread or pita, to serve (optional)

salad

8 oz. mixed leaves, washed and dried

1 tablespoon freshly squeezed lemon juice (a little less than ½ lemon)

¼ cup extra virgin olive oil

a metal pie plate or a deep ovenproof skillet, rubbed with olive oil

serves 4 as an appetizer: 2 as an entrée

This is not a traditional recipe. It's called a Greek omelet because all the ingredients are inspired by Greek cuisine. It is fast to make, nice to look at, and easy to eat. Serve hot or cold, with crusty bread or pita.

Arrange the tomatoes, pickled peppers, scallions, and olives equally around the oiled pan or pie plate. Crumble in the feta, then grind black pepper over the top. Sprinkle with parsley.

Put the eggs in a bowl, beat well, and season with a good pinch of salt. Pour the eggs over the ingredients in the pan. Bake in a preheated oven at 400°F until puffed and just golden around the edges, 15 to 20 minutes.

To make the salad, put the leaves in a bowl, add the lemon juice, oil, salt, and pepper. Toss well to mix, taste, and adjust the seasoning with more salt and pepper if necessary. Serve the omelet—hot, warm, or at room temperature—cut into wedges and accompanied by the salad and bread, if using.

risotto primavera

4 cups chicken or Vegetable Broth (see page 178)

1 stick butter

3 tablespoons olive oil

1 onion, finely chopped

1 garlic clove, chopped

1¼ cups arborio or carnaroli rice

1¼ lb. mixed green vegetables, such as asparagus, fava beans, green beans, runner beans, green cabbage, peas, or spinach, all chopped into even-size pieces

⅓ cup dry vermouth or white wine

a bunch of flat-leaf parsley, chopped

1¼ cups freshly grated Parmesan cheese

sea salt and freshly ground black pepper

serves 4

Pour the broth into a small saucepan and heat to simmering point.

Heat the butter and olive oil in a large saucepan. Add the onion and garlic and cook over low heat for 5 minutes until softened and translucent, but not browned. Add the rice, stirring with a wooden spoon to coat the grains thoroughly with butter and oil.

Add a ladle of hot broth to the rice, mix well, and let simmer. When the liquid has almost been absorbed by the rice, add another ladle of broth to the saucepan and stir constantly until it bubbles away. Continue, stirring the risotto as often as possible and adding more broth as needed.

After the risotto has been cooking for 12 minutes, add all the vegetables and stir well. Add the remaining broth, vermouth or wine, salt, and pepper. Cook, stirring, for another 4 to 5 minutes, then stir in the parsley and Parmesan. Cover, let rest for a couple of minutes, then serve.

moroccan shrimp *with couscous*

¼ cup extra virgin olive oil

2 teaspoons ground cumin

I teaspoon ground ginger

I teaspoon paprika

½ teaspoon cayenne pepper

2 lb. medium uncooked shrimp,
shell off

2 garlic cloves, crushed

2 lemons, I juiced, I cut
into wedges

a bunch of cilantro,
leaves finely chopped

coarse sea salt and freshly ground
black pepper

couscous

1¼ cups instant couscous,
about 8 oz.

½ teaspoon fine sea salt

3–4 tablespoons extra virgin
olive oil

freshly squeezed juice of ½ lemon

serves 4

Instant couscous couldn't be simpler or faster to prepare. The shrimp are a nicely spiced, quick little number to put on top, easily made in advance.

To prepare the couscous, put it in a large heatproof bowl, add ½ teaspoon salt, and mix. Add 1¾ cups boiling water and I tablespoon oil. Cover and set aside for 5 minutes. Meanwhile, bring some water to a boil in the bottom of a steamer. Transfer the couscous to the top compartment of the steamer, cover, and steam for 6 to 7 minutes. Fluff up with a fork and set aside.

Heat the oil in a sauté pan. Add the cumin, ginger, paprika, and cayenne and cook, stirring, for 30 seconds. Add the shrimp, garlic, and a good pinch of salt. Cook, stirring, for I minute. Squeeze in the juice of I lemon and add I cup water. Stir, then cover and simmer until the shrimp are opaque and cooked through, 3 to 5 minutes. Remove the pan from the heat and stir in the cilantro. Taste and adjust the seasoning with salt, pepper, and extra lemon juice if necessary.

Transfer the couscous to a serving plate. Season with the juice of ½ lemon and sprinkle with 2 to 3 tablespoons olive oil. Stir well. Put the shrimp on top, pour over their cooking juices, and serve with the lemon wedges.

green thai vegetable curry

This is a super-quick dish—it cooks just long enough for the vegetables to become tender.

Put the curry paste in a wok, heat, and cook for 2 minutes, stirring. Add the coconut milk, broth, and potato. Bring to a boil, reduce the heat, and simmer for 5 minutes. Add the broccoli and cauliflower florets, stalk end down, cover with a lid, and simmer for 4 minutes. Add the peas and sugar snaps and cook for another 2 minutes until all the vegetables are tender.

Ladle the curry into 4 bowls and serve with lime wedges and Thai fragrant rice.

3 tablespoons green
Thai curry paste

1¾ cups canned coconut milk

1¾ cups Vegetable Broth
(see page 178)

I large potato, peeled and
cut into 1-inch pieces

I cup broccoli florets

I cup cauliflower florets

I cup frozen peas

I cup sugar snap peas,
cut in half lengthwise

to serve

I lime, cut into wedges

cooked Thai fragrant rice

serves 4

1 large fennel bulb, with leafy tops

2 tablespoons olive oil

2 garlic cloves, crushed

¾ cup dry white wine

1¼ cups fish broth

4 cups canned chopped tomatoes (two 16-oz. cans)

a pinch of sugar

1 cup cherry tomatoes, cut in half

1 lb. monkfish fillet, cut into 1½-inch chunks

12 mussels, scrubbed*

12 large, unpeeled, uncooked shrimp

sea salt and freshly ground black pepper

to serve

extra virgin olive oil

crusty bread (optional)

serves 4

Shrimp shells are full of flavor, which seeps into the sauce and contributes to its richness. Eat this dish with your fingers and mop up with plenty of crusty fresh bread.

mediterranean fish stew

Remove the leafy tops from the fennel bulb, chop them coarsely, and set aside. Cut the bulb into quarters, remove and discard the core, then finely chop the bulb.

Heat the oil in a large saucepan or wok. Add the fennel bulb and sauté for 5 minutes. Add the garlic and sauté for another 1 minute. Add the wine, broth, canned tomatoes, and sugar and stir well. Bring to a boil, reduce the heat, then simmer for 5 minutes. Add the cherry tomatoes and cook for another 5 minutes. Add lots of salt and pepper.

Add the monkfish and return to a simmer. Stir in the mussels and shrimp, cover, and cook for about 5 minutes, or until the mussels have opened and the fish is cooked. Ladle the stew into deep plates or bowls. Sprinkle with the fennel tops and olive oil and serve with crusty bread, if using.

*Note To clean the mussels, scrub them and rinse in several changes of cold water. Pull off the beards or seaweed-like threads and discard any mussels that don't close when tapped against the counter—these are dead and inedible.

---

4 tablespoons butter

2 leeks, thinly sliced

4 oz. bacon, chopped

2¾ cups fish broth

4 oz. canned corn, drained and rinsed, about ½ cup

4 oz. potatoes, cut into small cubes

10 oz. smoked haddock, skinned (see recipe introduction)

1 tablespoon chopped fresh flat-leaf parsley

1 tablespoon chopped fresh chives

½ cup heavy cream

sea salt and freshly ground black pepper

thick slices of bread, to serve

serves 8

smoked fish chowder

This classic recipe is just perfect for cold days. Smoked haddock is produced on the East Coast but, if unavailable, use 7 oz. fresh haddock plus 3 oz. smoked salmon to add the smoky flavor.

Heat the butter in a large saucepan. Add the leeks and bacon and cook for 5 minutes, but do not brown. Add the fish broth and bring to a simmer. Add the corn, potatoes, and fish and cook for 10 minutes. Add salt and pepper to taste and bring to a gentle boil.

Just before serving, stir in the parsley, chives, and cream. Serve with thick slices of warm bread.

Watch the fillets carefully while cooking—they can easily overcook. Brushing the bars of the grill with a little oil will prevent the salmon from sticking.

grilled salmon fillets
with basil & parmesan butter

6 fresh salmon fillets

steamed seasonal vegetables, to serve (optional)

basil and parmesan butter

1½ sticks unsalted butter, softened

¼ cup freshly grated Parmesan cheese

1 teaspoon balsamic or sherry vinegar

¾ cup fresh basil leaves, sliced

freshly ground black pepper

marinade

1 large garlic clove, crushed

⅔ cup light olive oil

2 tablespoons balsamic or sherry vinegar

1–2 sprigs of thyme, crushed

serves 6

To make the basil and Parmesan butter, put the butter, Parmesan, vinegar, basil leaves, and black pepper, to taste, in a bowl and beat well. Scoop onto to a piece of wet wax paper and roll into a cylinder. Wrap in plastic and refrigerate (or freeze) for at least 1 hour, or until firm.

Put the marinade ingredients in a wide, shallow dish, mix well, then add the salmon fillets and turn to coat well. Cover and let marinate for 20 to 30 minutes. Remove the fillets from the marinade and pat dry with paper towels.

Heat an outdoor grill until the coals are MEDIUM hot and white (no longer red). Lightly oil the grill bars, add the salmon, and cook for about 3 minutes on each side until crisp and brown on the outside and just opaque all the way through—don't overcook it or the salmon will be dry. Alternatively, cook the salmon on a preheated stovetop grill pan. Serve the salmon fillets topped with slices of the chilled butter and with steamed seasonal vegetables, if using.

shrimp fried rice

This is a quick and easy dish to put together when you want something delicious but are short on time.

Heat the oil in a wok and swirl to coat. Add the garlic, ginger, and chile and stir-fry for 30 seconds. Add the shrimp, peas, scallions, and dried shrimp and stir-fry for 2 minutes until the shrimp turn pink.

Using a spatula, push the mixture to one side, add the eggs, and scramble until set. Then add the rice and stir over a high heat for 2 minutes until heated through.

Stir in the soy sauce, lemon juice, and cilantro, and serve.

*Note Asian dried shrimp are available in packages from Chinese markets. They keep very well in an airtight container if you don't use all of them.

2 tablespoons peanut or safflower oil

2 garlic cloves, chopped

1 inch fresh ginger, peeled and grated

1 fresh red chile, seeded and chopped

12 oz. small uncooked shrimp, peeled, deveined, and coarsely chopped

10 oz. frozen peas, about 2 cups, thawed

6 scallions, trimmed and sliced

¼ cup Asian dried shrimp*

2 eggs, lightly beaten

5 cups cooked Thai fragrant rice (from 1¾ cups uncooked rice)

3 tablespoons light soy sauce

freshly squeezed juice of ½ lemon

2 tablespoons chopped fresh cilantro

serves 4

chicken "panini" *with mozzarella*

8 oz. mozzarella cheese

4 large, skinless, boneless chicken breasts

8 large fresh basil leaves, plus extra to serve

2 garlic cloves, thinly sliced

1 tablespoon olive oil

sea salt and freshly ground black pepper

to serve

Salsa Rossa (see page 133)

mixed salad leaves

toothpicks

serves 4

Cut the mozzarella into 8 thick slices and set aside.

Put the chicken breasts onto a board and, using a sharp knife, cut horizontally through the breast without cutting all the way through. Open out flat and season the insides with a little salt and pepper.

Put 2 basil leaves, a few garlic slices, and 2 slices of cheese in each breast, then fold back over, pressing firmly together. Secure with toothpicks.

Brush the packages with a little oil and cook on a preheated outdoor grill or stovetop grill pan for about 8 minutes on each side until the chicken is cooked and the cheese is beginning to ooze at the sides. Serve hot with the salsa rossa, a few basil leaves, and mixed salad leaves.

Chicken is excellent poached in broth—the result is rich but healthy.
Keep the leftover broth in this recipe to use another time.

whole-grain mustard tarragon chicken

Strip the tarragon leaves from the stalks, reserve the leaves, and put the stalks and the broth in a large saucepan. Cover the pan with a lid and bring to a boil, then remove the lid and reduce the heat to a very gentle simmer, so the broth is barely moving.

Put the chicken breasts between 2 pieces of plastic wrap and, using a rolling pin, flatten each piece to $\frac{1}{2}$ inch thick. Remove and discard the plastic wrap.

Put the flattened chicken pieces in the stock and poach gently for about 15 minutes until firm to the touch and cooked through, with no trace of pink in the middle. Drain, reserving the broth for another recipe, and let the chicken cool a little. (The broth can be kept in the refrigerator for up to 3 days or frozen for up to 1 month.)

Meanwhile, coarsely chop the tarragon leaves and put them in a mini blender. Add all the dressing ingredients and 1 teaspoon water and blend until smooth.

Slice the chicken diagonally into thin strips. Divide the salad leaves between 4 large plates and top with the slices of chicken. Drizzle with the dressing and serve immediately with crusty bread.

4 large sprigs of tarragon

2 quarts chicken or Vegetable Broth (see page 178)

4 boneless, skinless chicken breasts

1 cup salad leaves

crusty bread, to serve

mustard dressing

¼ cup extra virgin olive oil

1 teaspoon whole-grain mustard

sea salt and freshly ground black pepper

serves 4

prosciutto-wrapped pork
with spinach & lentil salad

2 pork tenderloins, 12 oz. each

8 thin slices prosciutto

12 large fresh sage leaves, plus
1 tablespoon chopped fresh sage leaves

3 tablespoons extra virgin olive oil

4 shallots, finely chopped

1 garlic clove, crushed

2 cans lentils, 15 oz. each, about 4 cups,
drained, or 2 cups dried lentils, cooked

1/2 cup chicken broth

freshly squeezed juice of 1/2 lemon

4 oz. baby spinach leaves

sea salt and freshly ground black pepper

serves 4

Pork can easily become dry. The solution is not to cook it at too high a heat, and in this recipe the sage and prosciutto wrapping help to keep it moist, while adding flavor.

Cut the pork tenderloins in half crosswise to make 4 servings. Season with salt and pepper. Put 2 slices of prosciutto on a work surface, overlapping them slightly. Add 3 of the sage leaves in a line down the middle. Put a pork fillet on top and roll up, keeping the join underneath. Repeat with the remaining fillets.

Heat half the oil in a skillet, add the pork fillets seam side down, and sauté over medium heat for 12 to 15 minutes, turning frequently until evenly browned. Transfer to a warm oven and let rest for 5 minutes.

Meanwhile, add the remaining oil to the pan, add the shallots, garlic, and the chopped sage, and sauté for 3 minutes until softened but not golden. Add the lentils, chicken broth, and lemon juice and heat through for about 2 minutes. Stir in the spinach, cook until just wilted, then serve immediately with the pork.

---

1 tablespoon cumin seeds

1 tablespoon coriander seeds

1 tablespoon cracked black pepper

1/4 cup fresh flat-leaf parsley,
coarsely chopped

4 lamb steaks, from the leg,
6 oz. each

1 tablespoon olive oil

1 cup plain yogurt

3 tablespoons chopped fresh
mint leaves

1 teaspoon freshly squeezed
lemon juice

sea salt and freshly ground
black pepper

a stovetop grill pan

serves 4

Lamb can throw off quite a bit of fat as it cooks. The grill pan keeps the meat out of the fat, which you can just pour off as it accumulates.

lamb steaks *with coriander cumin crust*

Crush the cumin and coriander seeds coarsely with a mortar and pestle or the back of a wooden spoon. Add the black pepper and parsley and stir to mix. Rub the lamb steaks with the olive oil and coat each side with the parsley and spice mixture.

Heat a stovetop grill pan until hot, add the lamb, and cook for 2 to 3 minutes on each side for rare or 4 to 5 minutes for medium, depending on thickness.

While the lamb is cooking, put the yogurt, mint, and lemon juice in bowl, add salt and pepper to taste, and mix well. Carve the steaks into thick slices and serve with the minted yogurt.

linguine *with peas, pancetta, & sage*

2 cups shelled peas, fresh or frozen and thawed, about 10 oz.

4–5 tablespoons extra virgin olive oil

⅓ cup fresh bread crumbs

16 oz. linguine

3 oz. thinly sliced pancetta, chopped

3 garlic cloves, crushed

leaves from a few sprigs of sage, leaves finely chopped

⅓ cup dry white wine

¼ cup freshly grated Parmesan cheese

a small handful of fresh flat-leaf parsley, chopped

fine sea salt and freshly ground black pepper

serves 4–6

Lightly blanch the peas in a saucepan of boiling water for 2 to 3 minutes. Drain and set aside.

Heat 2 tablespoons of the oil in a skillet. Add the bread crumbs and cook until golden, stirring occasionally, about 3 minutes. Season lightly with salt and pepper and set aside.

Cook the pasta in a large saucepan of boiling, salted water until *al dente*, or according to the package instructions.

Heat 1 tablespoon oil in a saucepan large enough to hold all the pasta later. Add the pancetta and cook, stirring, until browned, 2 minutes. Add the garlic and cook, stirring, for 1 minute; don't let the garlic burn. Stir in the sage and wine. Cook, stirring, until the liquid has almost evaporated, about 1 minute. Set aside until needed.

Drain the cooked pasta thoroughly and add to the pan of pancetta. Add the peas and 1 to 2 tablespoons oil and cook over low heat, tossing well to mix. Stir in the cheese, parsley, and pepper; taste and add more salt and pepper, if necessary. Sprinkle with the toasted bread crumbs and serve hot.

peppered sage pork *with pasta*

2 sun-dried peppers

1 lb. pork tenderloin, sliced diagonally into 8 pieces

8 fresh sage leaves, plus 1 tablespoon chopped fresh sage leaves

8 oz. pappardelle or tagliatelle pasta

1 tablespoon butter

½ tablespoon olive oil

¼ cup dry sherry

¾ cup heavy cream

½ cup chicken broth

sea salt and freshly ground black pepper

serves 4

Soak the sun-dried peppers in boiling water according to the instructions on the package. Drain and cut into about 2-inch pieces.

Using the palm of your hand, gently flatten the pieces of pork into round, medallion shapes. Using a small, sharp knife, make 2 cuts through the center of each medallion. Thread a piece of sliced pepper through 1 cut and a sage leaf through the other on each medallion. Sprinkle with black pepper.

Cook the pasta in a saucepan of boiling, salted water until *al dente*, or according to the package instructions.

Meanwhile, heat the butter and oil in a nonstick skillet until foaming. Add the pork medallions and sauté over medium heat for 4 to 5 minutes on each side until golden and cooked through. Transfer to a warm plate, cover with foil, and set aside.

Pour the sherry into the hot skillet and boil for 30 seconds. Stir in the cream, broth, and sage. Bring to a boil again, reduce the heat, and simmer for 3 to 4 minutes. Add salt and pepper, to taste.

Drain the pasta, return it to the warm saucepan, and toss with half of the cream sauce. Divide between 4 serving plates. Top each serving with 2 pieces of pork and pour over the remaining sauce. Serve immediately.

CLASSIC DISHES

*There are certain dishes that every cook should have
in his or her culinary repertoire. These classics are
perfect for any occasion, whether you want
something comforting for just the two of you or
a tried-and-tested dish for a number of guests.
Chili with all the Trimmings is the answer if you
are entertaining a large group, while Pizza is
a welcome homemade treat for two.*

This meat sauce served with pasta is an all-time favorite. To make life easier, prepare double the quantity of sauce given here and freeze half for another time.

ragù

Heat the oil and butter in a heavy saucepan over medium heat. Add the carrot, celery, onion, and pancetta and cook until the onion is translucent. Increase the heat, add the meat, and sauté until browned. Add the wine and let it bubble until it has evaporated.

Lower the heat, add enough milk to cover the meat, then add the tomato paste and nutmeg. Simmer rapidly until the milk has reduced by at least half. Lower the heat, top up with enough warm broth or water to cover the meat, stir, cover with a lid, and simmer gently for at least 1 hour. Stir from time to time. Add salt and pepper to taste, then set aside to rest overnight to develop the flavors.

When ready to serve, reheat the sauce and add to the freshly cooked pasta. Stir in the Parmesan, parsley, and the 2 tablespoons butter and serve with extra Parmesan sprinkled over the top.

16 oz. long or short egg pasta, or rigatoni, freshly cooked

ragù sauce

1 tablespoon olive oil

2 tablespoons unsalted butter

1 small carrot, finely chopped

1 small celery stalk, finely chopped

1 small onion, finely chopped.

4 slices pancetta, prosciutto, or bacon, ground, about ½ cup

1 lb. ground beef, sirloin or round

2 tablespoons white wine

1½ cups whole milk, enough to cover the meat

1½ tablespoons tomato paste

½ nutmeg, freshly grated

1–2 cups hot Vegetable Broth (see page 178) or water

sea salt and freshly ground black pepper

to serve

½ cup freshly grated Parmesan cheese, plus extra to taste

3 tablespoons chopped fresh flat-leaf parsley

2 tablespoons unsalted butter

serves 4–6

---

16 oz. pasta, such as spaghetti or penne, freshly cooked

carbonara sauce

2 whole eggs

5 egg yolks (to separate eggs, see page 147)

2 tablespoons unsalted butter

½ cup light cream

½ cup freshly grated Parmesan cheese, plus extra to serve

8 oz. pancetta, prosciutto, or bacon, about 8 slices

olive oil, for sautéing

1 garlic clove, crushed

freshly ground black pepper

serves 4–6

carbonara

Crisp, garlic-scented bacon with a stream of creamy fresh eggs setting in the warm pasta—an Italian classic.

Put the eggs and egg yolks in a bowl and mix lightly with a fork. Add the butter, cream, grated Parmesan, and lots of black pepper. Let stand without mixing.

Chop the pancetta into slivers. Cover the base of a medium skillet with olive oil and heat. When it starts to haze, add the pancetta. When the fat starts to run, add the crushed garlic and stir well. Continue sautéing until the pancetta becomes crisp and golden.

Add the pancetta and pan juices to the freshly cooked pasta and mix vigorously. Beat the egg mixture lightly with a fork and pour it over the pasta. Mix well and serve at once, with extra Parmesan and plenty of black pepper—the butter will melt and the eggs will cook in the heat of the pasta.

tomato pizza
with capers & anchovies

If you are making fresh pizza bases, cook the pizzas one at a time and share them straight from the oven as soon as they are ready.

1 recipe Pizza Dough (see page 185),
2 packages pizza crust mix (6½ oz. each),
or 1 package frozen pizza dough (16 oz.), cut in half
all-purpose flour, for dusting
2 large ripe tomatoes, chopped
2 tablespoons capers, rinsed and drained
12 anchovy fillets in oil, drained and chopped
8 oz. fresh mozzarella cheese, chopped
a few fresh basil leaves
sea salt and freshly ground black pepper

a pizza stone or baking sheet

serves 2

If using pizza crust mix, prepare the dough according to the directions on the package. Put the dough in a bowl and let rise until doubled in size.

Preheat the oven to its highest setting, about 500°F, and put a pizza stone or baking sheet on the top shelf to heat.

Divide the risen dough in half and transfer one half to a well-floured surface. Roll it out to 12 inches diameter. Take the hot stone or baking sheet from the oven and carefully put the pizza base on top.

Add half the tomatoes, half the capers, half the anchovies, half the mozzarella, and top with a few basil leaves. Season with salt and pepper, to taste.

Bake in the preheated oven for 10 to 12 minutes until bubbling and golden. Serve at once, then repeat to make a second pizza.

arugula, bresaola,
& parmesan topping

3 plum tomatoes, sliced crosswise
1 teaspoon sugar
extra virgin olive oil, for sprinkling
1½ cups arugula
8 slices bresaola or prosciutto, torn into pieces
⅔ cup fresh Parmesan cheese shavings
freshly ground black pepper

Make the pizza dough, divide it in half, then roll it out as in the main recipe, left. Arrange the tomato slices on top of the 2 pizza bases and sprinkle with the sugar, salt, pepper, and olive oil. Bake, one at a time, as in the main recipe. Remove from the oven, top with half the arugula, half the bresaola, and half the Parmesan. Sprinkle with oil and black pepper. Serve at once, then repeat to make a second pizza.

feta, onion, parsley,
& lemon topping

3 plum tomatoes, sliced crosswise
1 teaspoon sugar
1½ cups feta cheese, crumbled into large chunks
½ red onion, finely chopped
a large handful of fresh flat-leaf parsley
2 tablespoons extra virgin olive oil, plus extra for sprinkling
1 tablespoon freshly squeezed lemon juice
sea salt and freshly ground black pepper

Make the pizza dough, divide it in half, then roll it out as in the main recipe, left. Arrange the tomato slices on top of the 2 pizza bases and sprinkle with the sugar, salt, pepper, and olive oil. Bake the first pizza crust as in the main recipe. Meanwhile, put the feta, onion, parsley, olive oil, and lemon juice in a bowl and mix well. Remove the pizza crust from the oven, spread half the feta mixture over the top and serve at once. Repeat to make a second pizza.

There may seem a lot of mustard in this sauce, but, when you cook mustard, it loses its heat and you are left with a delicious flavor which no one can quite place once the poaching liquid has been added.

traditional fish pie

Put the milk in a wide saucepan, heat just to boiling point, then add the fish. Turn off the heat and poach until opaque—do not overcook.

Meanwhile, melt 1¼ sticks of the butter in another saucepan, then stir in the mustard powder and flour. Remove the pan from the heat and strain the poaching liquid from the fish into the pan.

Arrange the fish and eggs in a shallow pie dish or casserole.

Return the pan to the heat and, beating vigorously to smooth out any lumps, bring the mixture to a boil. Season with salt and pepper, if necessary. (Take care: if you are using smoked fish, it may be salty enough.) Pour the sauce over the fish and eggs and mix carefully.

Cook the potatoes in boiling salted water until tender, then drain. Return to the pan. Melt the remaining butter in a small saucepan. Reserve ¼ cup of this butter and stir the remainder into the potatoes. Mash well and season with salt and pepper. Spoon the potatoes carefully over the sauced fish, then brush the surface generously with the reserved butter. Transfer the pie to a preheated oven at 400°F for 20 minutes, or until nicely browned.

Note If no finnan haddie is available, add 4 oz. smoked salmon, thinly sliced, to the poached fish just before adding the sauce.

2 cups milk

1½ lb. finnan haddie or fresh haddock, skinned

2¾ sticks unsalted butter

1 tablespoon dry mustard powder

¼ cup all-purpose flour

2 hard-cooked eggs, peeled and quartered

2 lb. baking potatoes, peeled and cut into even-size pieces

sea salt and freshly ground black pepper

a shallow ovenproof dish or casserole

serves 4

Cooking fish

- *It's important not to overcook fish—cook it just until it becomes opaque all the way through.*

- *Remember it keeps cooking after you remove it from the pan.*

- *Tuna can be served pink in the middle, but it must be very fresh. To make sure, buy it from a fishmonger.*

coq au vin

4 boneless, skinless chicken breasts

⅔ cup red wine

1 garlic clove, sliced

2 tablespoons olive oil

a sprig of thyme, plus 4 sprigs to serve

sauce

1 oz. dried porcini mushrooms, rinsed thoroughly

1 tablespoon olive oil

6 shallots, cut in half

a pinch of sugar

4 oz. bacon, chopped

1 garlic clove, crushed

2 teaspoons all-purpose flour

⅔ cup red wine

⅔ cup port

a sprig of thyme

sea salt and freshly ground black pepper

a stovetop grill pan

serves 4

This modern version of the classic dish of chicken cooked in wine is a handy shortcut. Cutting slashes in the chicken lets the marinade soak into and flavor the meat, while keeping it tender and moist.

Using a small, sharp knife, slash the top of each chicken breast in a crisscross fashion, taking care not to cut all the way through. Put the breasts in a shallow dish. Add the red wine, garlic, oil, and a sprig of thyme and mix. Cover and refrigerate for 20 minutes. The chicken will absorb most of the marinade.

Meanwhile, to make the sauce, put the dried porcini in a heatproof bowl and cover with ⅔ cup boiling water. Let soak for 15 minutes, then drain, reserving the liquid. (The liquid can sometimes be gritty, so strain it through a tea strainer.) Coarsely chop the mushrooms.

Heat the oil in a skillet. Add the shallots and sugar and sauté for about 10 minutes until golden. Add the bacon and garlic and sauté for a further 5 minutes. Stir in the flour and cook for 1 minute. Add the mushrooms and their soaking liquid, red wine, port, and a sprig of thyme. Bring to a boil, reduce the heat, and simmer for 20 minutes until syrupy. Add salt and pepper to taste.

Meanwhile, heat a stovetop grill pan until hot. Transfer the chicken to the grill pan, discarding any remaining marinade. Cook for about 5 minutes on each side, until the chicken is cooked through, with no trace of pink in the middle. Serve the chicken with the sauce poured over and topped with a sprig of thyme.

Chicken cooking tips

- *It's important to cook chicken all the way through. To test, push a skewer or small sharp knife into the thickest part. The juices that run out should be clear or golden— if they are pink or bloody, you must cook it for longer.*

- *To check whether chicken breasts are cooked, cut one to see. Cut through the thickest part—it should be opaque all the way through, with no trace of blood.*

- *Boneless, skinless chicken is quick and easy to cook, but if you cook it with the skin on and the bone in, it will have more flavor. Skin keeps it moist, while the bone helps conduct heat.*

tex-mex ribs

2 racks spareribs, I lb. each

Chile-Spiked Cornbread, to serve
(see below)

sweet chile marinade

2 garlic cloves, crushed

2 tablespoons sea salt

2 tablespoons ground cumin

2 teaspoons chilli powder

I teaspoon dried oregano

½ cup maple syrup or honey

¼ cup red wine vinegar

¼ cup olive oil

serves 4-6

Nibbling away at succulent grilled pork ribs is one of the true pleasures of a cookout. Here spareribs are marinated in a mix of spices and maple syrup giving them an authentic sweet-hot flavor.

Wash the ribs and pat them dry with paper towels. Transfer to a shallow, non-metal dish.

Put all the marinade ingredients in a bowl and mix well. Pour it over the ribs, then work in well with your hands. Cover and let marinate overnight in the refrigerator.

The next day, return the ribs to room temperature for I hour, then cook on a preheated medium-hot outdoor grill for about 30 minutes, turning and basting frequently with the marinade juices. Let cool slightly, then serve with chile-spiked cornbread.

I¼ cups medium cornmeal

I¼ cups all-purpose flour

I½ teaspoons salt

I tablespoon baking powder

2 eggs, beaten

I cup milk

2 tablespoons olive oil

2 large red chile peppers, such as Anaheim
or New Mexico, seeded and chopped

I cup canned corn kernels, drained

¼ cup finely grated Cheddar cheese

2 tablespoons chopped fresh cilantro

*a cake pan, 8 inches square, greased and
bottom-lined with parchment paper*

serves 8

chile-spiked cornbread

This is a great quickbread, ideal for picnics. It is easy to make and can be eaten as a snack or as part of a meal.

Put the cornmeal, flour, salt, and baking powder in a bowl and mix. Make a well in the center and pour in the eggs, milk, and olive oil. Beat with a wooden spoon to make a smooth batter.

Fold in the chile peppers, corn, cheese, and cilantro, then spoon the mixture into the prepared cake pan. Bake in a preheated oven at 400°F for 25 minutes, or until a skewer inserted in the center comes out clean.

Remove from the oven and let cool in the pan for about 5 minutes, then invert onto a wire rack to cool completely. Cut into squares to serve.

The combination of orange, tomato, and chile gives this dish a more Spanish than Italian flavor, but the sauce is only lightly spiced, making it a good choice for younger guests (omit the cayenne altogether if you prefer). The sauce and/or meatballs can easily be made a day ahead; in fact, it's better that way. Serve with a red Rioja and roasted or sautéed potatoes. Any leftovers make a great sandwich filling, stuffed in a baguette, wrapped in foil, and warmed in the oven.

meatballs in red bell pepper sauce

1 cup fresh bread crumbs

3 tablespoons milk

1 small onion, finely chopped

a handful of fresh flat-leaf parsley leaves, chopped

2 garlic cloves, finely chopped

1¾ lb. ground meat, preferably a mixture of beef and pork

1½ teaspoons fine sea salt

1 teaspoon dried oregano

1 teaspoon ground cumin

½ teaspoon sweet smoked paprika

1 egg, beaten

3 tablespoons extra virgin olive oil

red bell pepper sauce

2 red bell peppers

2 tablespoons extra virgin olive oil, plus extra for rubbing

several sprigs of thyme

1 bay leaf

1 onion, grated

6 garlic cloves, crushed

¼ teaspoon cayenne pepper (optional)

⅓ cup red wine

½ unwaxed orange, well scrubbed

32 oz. tomato purée

sea salt and freshly ground black pepper

aluminum foil

a baking sheet

kitchen twine

a baking dish (see method)

makes about 25 meatballs

To make the red bell pepper sauce, rub the bell peppers with olive oil, then put them on a sheet of foil on a baking sheet (make the piece of foil large enough to fold over and enclose the peppers after roasting). Roast in a preheated oven at 425°F until tender and charred, 30 to 40 minutes. Remove from the oven, enclose in the foil, and set aside to loosen the skin. When cool enough to handle, about 30 minutes, remove the skins and seeds, chop the flesh coarsely, and set aside. Lower the oven temperature to 400°F.

Meanwhile, tie the thyme and bay leaf together with kitchen twine. Heat 2 tablespoons of the oil in a skillet. Add the onion and a pinch of salt and cook until soft, about 2 minutes. Add the garlic and cayenne, if using, and cook, stirring, for 1 minute. Stir in the wine and squeeze in the orange juice (reserve the rest of the orange) and cook for 30 seconds. Add the tomato purée, a good pinch of salt, the bunch of herbs, and the reserved orange half. Simmer gently until thick, 20 to 30 minutes. Add salt and pepper to taste. Stir in the red bell peppers, remove the herbs and orange, and transfer to a baking dish large enough to hold the meatballs in a single layer. This sauce can be made a day ahead.

To make the meatballs, put the bread crumbs, milk, onion, parsley, garlic, ground meat, salt, oregano, cumin, paprika, and beaten egg in a large bowl. Mix well (your hands are best). Shape spoonfuls of the meat mixture into balls, just slightly larger than a golf ball. Set on a tray.

To cook, heat the 3 tablespoons oil in a large, heavy skillet. Working in batches, cook the meatballs until browned evenly, about 5 minutes per batch—don't worry if they don't stay perfectly formed. Using a slotted spoon, transfer the browned meatballs to the sauce in the baking dish. When all the meatballs are browned, gently spoon some sauce over each one, then cover the baking dish with foil, and bake for 20 minutes in the preheated oven. Serve hot.

The classic version of this dish is pasta layered with meat sauce and creamy "salsa besciamella." It is very easy to assemble. Make the ragù the day before, and the besciamella sauce on the day. Just make sure the meat sauce is quite liquid. This will be absorbed into the pasta as it cooks. Vary the recipe by replacing the meat sauce with a mixture of ricotta cheese, spinach, chopped sun-dried tomatoes, Parmesan cheese, and herbs.

lasagne

about 12 sheets dried lasagne verdi

about ½ cup freshly grated
Parmesan cheese

sea salt and freshly ground black pepper

besciamella sauce

12 tablespoons butter

⅔ cup all-purpose flour

about 4 cups milk

ragù

3 oz. pancetta or dry-cure smoked
bacon in a piece

4 oz. chicken livers

4 tablespoons butter

1 medium onion, finely chopped

1 medium carrot, chopped

1 celery stalk, trimmed and
finely chopped

8 oz. lean ground beef

2 tablespoons tomato paste

¼ cup dry white wine

¾ cup beef broth or water

freshly grated nutmeg

*a deep baking dish,
10 x 8 inches, buttered*

serves 4–6

To make the besciamella, melt the butter in a medium saucepan. When foaming, add the flour and cook over gentle heat for about 5 minutes without letting it brown. Have a balloon whisk ready. Slide the pan off the heat and add all the milk at once, whisking very well. When all the flour and butter have been amalgamated and there are no lumps, return to the heat and slowly bring to a boil, whisking all the time. When it comes to a boil, add salt, simmer gently for 2 to 3 minutes, then use immediately.

If making in advance, cover the surface directly with plastic wrap to prevent a skin forming, then let cool. When reheating, remove the plastic and reheat very gently, stirring every now and then until liquid. Don't worry too much about lumps—they will disappear when the whole dish cooks. If you like a thinner sauce, just add extra milk after it has boiled and thickened.

To make the ragù, cut the pancetta into small cubes. Trim the chicken livers, removing any fat or gristle. Cut off any discolored bits, which will be bitter if left on. Coarsely chop the livers.

Melt the butter in a saucepan, add the pancetta, and cook for 2 to 3 minutes until browning. Add the onion, carrot, and celery and brown these too. Stir in the ground beef and brown until just changing color, but not hardening—break it up with a wooden spoon. Stir in the chicken livers and cook for 2 to 3 minutes. Add the tomato paste, mix well, and pour in the wine and broth. Season well with nutmeg, salt, and pepper. Bring to a boil, cover, and simmer very gently for as long as you can—2 hours if possible.

Cook the sheets of dried lasagne in plenty of boiling water in batches according to the package instructions. Lift out with a slotted spoon and drain on a clean dish towel.

Spoon one-third of the meat sauce into a buttered baking dish. Cover with 4 sheets of lasagne and spread with one-third of the besciamella. Repeat twice more, finishing with a layer of besciamella covering the whole top. Sprinkle with Parmesan cheese. Bake in a preheated oven at 350°F for about 45 minutes until brown and bubbling. Let stand for 10 minutes to settle and firm up before serving.

Forget the stuff that's slopped on baked potatoes—this is the real thing, made with finely chopped chuck steak instead of hamburger and spiced with several types of chile, not the ubiquitous chilli powder from the supermarket shelf. That said, maybe Texas cowboys didn't put red wine in their chili, but surely they'd approve of the addition. The various bits to put on at the end are also fairly urban, but they fill out the table nicely and add to the enjoyment.

chili *with all the trimmings*

Put the chipotle in a small heatproof bowl and just cover with hot water. Let soak for at least 15 minutes, or as long as it takes to prepare all the other ingredients.

Heat 2 tablespoons of the oil in a large saucepan. Add the peppers, onion, celery, green chile, and a good pinch of salt and cook until soft, 5 to 7 minutes, stirring frequently. Remove from the pan and set aside. Raise the heat under the pan, add the remaining 2 tablespoons of the oil, and the meat. Cook, stirring frequently, until browned, 1 to 2 minutes. Add the garlic and another pinch of salt and cook, stirring constantly, for 1 minute. Add the wine, bring to a boil and cook for 1 minute.

Return the pepper and onion mixture to the pan and stir in the red pepper flakes, cumin, and oregano. Add the tomatoes, beans, bay leaf, and a good pinch of salt and stir well. Remove the chipotle from the soaking liquid, chop finely, and stir into the pan, along with the soaking liquid. Cover and simmer gently until the meat is tender, 15 to 20 minutes. Add salt and pepper to taste.

At this point, the chili is ready, but you should set it aside for at least 2 to 3 hours before serving to develop the flavors or, ideally, make 1 day in advance and chill until needed. When ready to serve, remove the bay leaf, reheat the chili and serve hot, with all the trimmings in separate bowls.

1 dried chipotle chile

$\frac{1}{4}$ cup extra virgin olive oil

4 bell peppers (1 red, 1 yellow, 1 orange, 1 green), cut in half, seeded, and chopped

1 large onion

2 celery stalks, chopped

$\frac{1}{2}$–1 fresh green chile, finely chopped

1$\frac{3}{4}$ lb. chuck steak, cut into small cubes

3 garlic cloves, chopped

1 cup red wine, fresh beef broth, or water

$\frac{1}{4}$ teaspoon hot red pepper flakes

2 teaspoons ground cumin

2 teaspoons dried oregano

28 oz. canned chopped tomatoes

42 oz. canned red kidney beans (3 cans, 14 oz. each), drained and rinsed

1 bay leaf

coarse sea salt and freshly ground black pepper

to serve

1–2 ripe avocados, chopped and tossed with lime juice

a bunch of scallions, chopped

a bunch of cilantro, chopped

8–12 tortillas (at least 2 per person), warmed

sour cream

freshly grated cheese, such as mild Cheddar

lime wedges

Tabasco sauce

serves 6-8

These wedges have a delicious spice mix coating that makes them the ideal partner for steak or simple roasts. Even better, add some crushed garlic to a bowl of mayonnaise and use as a dip.

potato wedges
with garlic & paprika

3 lb. potatoes, unpeeled but well scrubbed

1 bay leaf

1/3 cup extra virgin olive oil

3 garlic cloves, finely chopped

1 tablespoon dried oregano

1 teaspoon sweet smoked Spanish paprika

a handful of flat-leaf parsley, chopped

coarse sea salt and freshly ground black pepper

a baking sheet

serves 4

If the potatoes are large, cut in half lengthwise, otherwise leave them whole. Put them in a large saucepan of water with the bay leaf. Bring the water to a boil, add a heaping tablespoon of coarse salt, and cook until just tender, but not completely soft. Drain and let cool slightly.

When the potatoes are cool enough to handle, cut into wedges. Put in a large dish and add the oil, garlic, oregano, paprika, and salt and mix well with your hands until evenly coated.

Arrange the wedges in a single layer on a baking sheet and bake in a preheated oven at 450°F until browned, 30 to 40 minutes. Sprinkle with pepper and parsley and serve hot.

french fries

1 lb. potatoes, suitable for baking and frying

safflower oil, for frying

sea salt

a large saucepan with frying basket, or an electric deep-fryer

serves 4

Peel the potatoes and cut into ¼-inch slices. Cut the slices into ¼-inch strips. Put the strips into a bowl of ice water for at least 5 minutes. When ready to cook, drain well and pat dry with paper towels.

Fill a large saucepan one-third full with the oil or, if using a deep-fryer, to the manufacturer's recommended level. Heat the oil to 375°F or until a cube of bread will brown in 30 seconds. Working in batches, put 2 large handfuls of potato strips in the frying basket, lower carefully into the oil, and fry for about 4 minutes. Remove and drain on paper towels. Repeat until all the strips have been cooked.

Skim any debris off the top of the oil, reheat the oil to 375°F, then fry the strips, in batches, for a second time until crisp and golden, about 2 minutes. Remove from the oil and drain on paper towels, then sprinkle with salt. Serve immediately.

This French classic dish is a much more sophisticated version of macaroni and cheese. It is ideal for serving with beef stews, as the gratin is even better when mixed with broth.

macaroni gratin

10 oz. thin macaroni

2 cups milk

3 tablespoons sour cream
or crème fraîche

4 tablespoons unsalted butter

¼ cup all-purpose flour

1⅔ cups finely grated Beaufort cheese, 7 oz.*

coarse sea salt and freshly ground black pepper

a baking dish, 12 inches long, buttered

serves 6

Cook the macaroni in plenty of boiling, well-salted water according to the instructions on the package. Drain and rinse well.

Heat the milk in the rinsed saucepan and stir in the sour cream. Melt the butter in a second saucepan over medium-high heat. Stir in the flour and cook, stirring constantly, for 3 minutes. Pour in the milk mixture and stir constantly until the mixture thickens. Season with salt and pepper.

Stir the macaroni into the milk mixture and taste, adding salt and pepper if necessary. Transfer to the prepared baking dish and sprinkle with the cheese. Cook under a preheated broiler until bubbling and browned, 10 to 15 minutes. Serve hot.

*Note Beaufort is an Alpine cheese, similar to Gruyère, but with a slightly sweeter, more pronounced nutty flavor. It is becoming more widely available outside France, but if you cannot find it, Emmental, Cantal, or any firm, Cheddar-like cheese will do.

Choose large "old" potatoes—the sort that become fluffy when mashed. When boiling potatoes, it's always important to add salt to the water before cooking.

classic creamy mashed potatoes

2 lb. large "old" potatoes, such as baking potatoes, peeled and cut into 2-inch cubes

about ⅔ cup milk, preferably hot

3 tablespoons butter

sea salt and freshly ground black pepper

serves 4

Put the potatoes in a medium saucepan. Cover with cold water and add a pinch of salt.

Bring to a boil, reduce the heat, half-cover with a lid, and simmer for 15 to 20 minutes until tender when pierced with a knife. Drain and return the potatoes to the pan.

Return the saucepan to the heat and mash the potatoes with a fork or potato masher for 30 seconds—this will steam off any excess water.

Stir in the milk and butter, then mash until smooth, adding extra milk, if necessary. Season to taste with salt and pepper. Serve immediately.

Mashed potato tips

- *Best for mashing are large "old" potatoes (often called floury or baking potatoes). They become light and fluffy when boiled.*

- *Cut them into even-size pieces, so they will cook at the same rate and all be ready at the same time.*

- *Always start them in COLD water. Bring to a boil, then simmer—with the lid slightly ajar—until tender when pierced with the point of a knife.*

- *Never use a food processor to mash your potatoes— you'll end up with wallpaper glue.*

SPECIAL OCCASIONS

Forget the rushed meals during the week, on certain occasions you will want to prepare something extra-special for your loved one. Whether it's your anniversary, birthday, or Valentine's Day, or simply because you want to give your partner a treat, here are some great ideas for you to try. Oysters make a romantic start to a meal for two. Follow these with Beef en Croûte and finish with a decadent dessert, such as Raspberry Roulade from page 147.

seared scallops
with brittle prosciutto

Scallops cook fast, and carry on cooking off the heat, so keep a careful watch on them—when overcooked, they are tough.

4 slices of prosciutto

12 large scallops

about 2 cups salad leaves such as mâche or baby spinach

freshly ground black pepper

to drizzle

extra virgin olive oil

balsamic vinegar

a stovetop grill pan

serves 4

Heat a stovetop grill pan until very hot. Add the prosciutto and cook for 1 to 2 minutes on each side until crisp. Remove from the pan and set aside.

Grind black pepper over the scallops, then add them to the hot pan. Cook for 1 to 2 minutes on each side until opaque.

Divide the salad leaves between 4 plates. Lightly drizzle with oil and a little balsamic vinegar.

Top each serving of salad with 3 scallops, then break the brittle prosciutto over the top. Sprinkle with black pepper and serve at once.

oysters rockefeller

This adaptation of the classic dish—invented in New Orleans in the 1890s—makes a decadent appetizer when served with champagne.

1 shallot, finely chopped

1 small garlic clove, crushed

1 small piece of fennel, finely chopped

6 tablespoons unsalted butter

½ cup heavy cream

3 sprigs of flat-leaf parsley

4 sprigs of chervil

4 sprigs of watercress

2 teaspoons Pernod

24 fresh oysters in the shell

a large pinch of cayenne pepper

⅓ cup fresh bread crumbs

6 tablespoons freshly grated Parmesan cheese

sea salt and freshly ground black pepper

a broiler pan, lined with foil

serves 6

Put the shallot, garlic, fennel, and butter in a skillet, heat gently, and cook until softened and translucent. Add the cream and simmer for 2 minutes. Remove from the heat. Remove the leaves from the parsley, chervil, and watercress sprigs, chop them and add to the pan along with the Pernod.

To shuck the oysters, hold them firmly in one hand (you can wrap that hand in a dish towel, for safety reasons, if you like). Insert a knife into the hinge of the shell and twist it until the top shell is loosened, then twist it off. Loosen each oyster from both sides of its shell with a knife and leave it in the deepest shell. Arrange the flat shells on the foil-lined broiler pan and balance the round shells on top. Put 1 teaspoon of the herb mixture on top of each oyster.

Put the cayenne, bread crumbs, Parmesan, salt, and pepper in a bowl and mix. Sprinkle 1 teaspoon of the herb mixture on top of each oyster. Cook under a preheated hot broiler until just golden, 30–60 seconds. Serve immediately; the idea is not to cook the oysters but to keep a hot-cold contrast.

The garlicky, saffron-scented sauce used here is a slightly more flavorsome departure from the classic French mussel recipe with shallots and white wine, called "à la marinière."

mussels *with fennel, tomatoes, garlic, & saffron*

2 tablespoons extra virgin olive oil
1 small onion, chopped
½ fennel bulb, chopped
4 garlic cloves, crushed
1 cup dry white wine
2 cups canned chopped peeled tomatoes, 16 oz.
a pinch of saffron threads
2 lb. fresh mussels
coarse sea salt
a handful of fresh flat-leaf parsley, chopped, to serve

serves 4

Heat the oil in a large sauté pan. Add the onion and fennel and cook until soft, 3 to 5 minutes. Add the garlic, wine, and tomatoes. Boil for 1 minute, then lower the heat, add the saffron and a pinch of salt. Simmer gently for 15 minutes.

Just before serving, clean and debeard the mussels, discarding any that do not close. (To clean mussels, see note on page 59.)

Raise the heat under the sauce and, when it boils, add the prepared mussels. Cover the pan and cook until the mussels open, 2 to 3 minutes. Discard any that do not open. Sprinkle with parsley and serve immediately.

Variation French fries are the classic accompaniment for mussels when served as an entrée. See the recipe on page 87.

smoked wild salmon & scrambled eggs *with "caviar"*

Use caviar if you are wildly rich—and try the scrambled eggs made with duck eggs. These are available from some gourmet stores and farmstands.

8 hen eggs or 4 duck eggs
½ cup milk
4 tablespoons butter
8 slices whole-wheat bread
8 oz. smoked salmon, sliced
3 oz. caviar or salmon caviar (optional)
sea salt and white pepper
a bunch of chives, to serve

serves 8

Break the eggs into a bowl and beat lightly. Add the milk and beat again. Melt the butter in a nonstick saucepan, then add the eggs and salt and pepper to taste. Cook, stirring constantly with a wooden spoon, for 5 to 8 minutes, until softly scrambled. Remove the pan from the heat just before the eggs are done, as they will carry on cooking when they are off the heat.

Warm the bread in a preheated oven at 350°F for 10 minutes, then transfer to serving plates. Spoon the scrambled eggs onto the toast and top with smoked salmon. Add a teaspoon of caviar, if using, and serve at once, topped with a few chives.

tuna *with paprika crumbs*

Tuna takes well to hot paprika seasoning. The topping gives a moist and crunchy texture to a fish that can become dry and overcooked only too easily.

To make the romesco sauce, char the peppers under a preheated hot broiler, put them in a paper bag, seal, and let steam for 10 minutes. Remove the skin, seeds, and membranes. Heat 1 teaspoon of the oil in a nonstick pan, lightly brown the garlic, then add the chile and tomatoes. Dry out the mixture over high heat so it starts to fry and even brown a little. Transfer to a blender, add the peppers, vinegar, and remaining oil, and purée until smooth. Stir in the nuts to thicken the sauce and add salt to taste.

To make the paprika topping, heat the oil in a skillet, add the bread crumbs, basil, paprika, tomato paste, sugar, and ½ teaspoon salt. Stir well and sauté until crunchy. Remove from the pan and let cool.

Season the tuna with salt and pepper, put on the oiled baking sheet, and roast in a preheated oven at 500°F for 5 minutes. Remove from the oven and turn over the steaks. Pile the paprika bread crumbs on top, then add the slice of cheese, if using. Return to the oven and cook for a further 5 minutes or until the cheese has melted. Serve on a bed of buttered spinach or arugula salad, with romesco sauce served separately.

4 tuna steaks, 6 oz. each

1½ oz. Cheddar cheese, cut into 4 thin slices (optional)

sea salt and freshly ground black pepper

buttered spinach or arugula salad, to serve

romesco sauce

2 red bell peppers

½ cup olive oil

2 garlic cloves

1 fresh red chile, seeded and sliced

7 oz. canned plum tomatoes

1½ tablespoons red wine vinegar

1 tablespoon ground hazelnuts

1 tablespoon ground almonds

paprika bread crumb crunch

1 tablespoon olive oil

1 cup fresh white bread crumbs

1 tablespoon chopped fresh basil leaves

½ teaspoon hot smoked Spanish paprika

1 teaspoon tomato paste

½ teaspoon sugar

a baking sheet, oiled

serves 4

sole meunière

Put some flour on a large plate, add the fish, cover with flour on both sides, and shake off the excess.

Reserve 2 tablespoons of the butter. Heat the oil and remaining butter over medium-high heat in a nonstick skillet large enough to hold both fish side by side. When it sizzles, add the sole and cook for about 3 minutes. Turn them over and cook on the other side for 3 minutes. Sprinkle the first side with salt while the second side is cooking.

When the fish is cooked through, transfer to warmed serving plates and season the second side with salt.

Return the skillet to the heat, add the remaining 2 tablespoons butter, and melt over high heat. When it begins to sizzle, lower the heat and add the lemon juice. Cook, scraping the pan for about 10 seconds; do not let the butter burn. Pour this lemon butter over the fish and sprinkle with parsley. Serve immediately with lemon slices.

all-purpose flour

2 soles, about 10 oz., skinned and cleaned

4 tablespoons unsalted butter

2 tablespoons safflower oil

freshly squeezed juice of ½ lemon

fine sea salt

to serve

a handful of fresh flat-leaf parsley, finely chopped

½ lemon, thinly sliced

serves 2

Serve these delicious duck breasts with sautéed or roasted potatoes and a good bottle of red wine.

duck breasts *with peppercorns*

Trim the excess fat from around the duck breasts, then score the skin in a diamond pattern.

Heat a heavy skillet. When hot, add the duck skin side down and cook 7 to 8 minutes. Turn and cook the other side 4 to 5 minutes, depending on thickness. Remove from the pan, season with salt, and keep them warm.

Drain almost all the fat from the pan. Return to the heat and add the Cognac, scraping the bottom of the pan. Stir in the cream, black pepper, and green peppercorns. Warm through, but don't let the sauce boil.

Slice the duck diagonally lengthwise and put on warm serving plates. Pour the sauce over the top and serve immediately with your choice of potatoes.

2 duck breasts, about 1½ lb.

3 tablespoons Cognac

1 cup sour cream or crème fraîche

1 tablespoon coarsely ground black pepper

1 tablespoon green peppercorns in brine, drained

coarse sea salt

sautéed or roasted potatoes, to serve

serves 2

chicken, asparagus, & gorgonzola salad *with hazelnuts*

8 oz. mixed salad leaves, such as frisée, baby spinach, or arugula

4 tablespoons extra virgin olive oil

1½ lb. thin asparagus spears, 10–12 per person

4 boneless, skinless chicken breasts

4 oz. Gorgonzola cheese, cut into 4 slices

2 tablespoons coarsely crushed hazelnuts

fine sea salt and freshly ground black pepper

dressing

3 tablespoons freshly squeezed orange juice

1 teaspoon Dijon mustard

½ teaspoon fine sea salt

8 tablespoons extra virgin olive oil, ½ cup

parchment paper

a stovetop grill pan

serves 4

To make the dressing, put the orange juice, mustard, and salt in a small bowl and beat with a fork or whisk until blended. Add the oil, a spoonful at a time, beating until thick. Season with pepper. Put all the salad leaves in a bowl, add half the dressing, and toss well. Divide the leaves between 4 serving plates and set aside.

Heat 2 tablespoons of the oil in a large, nonstick skillet. Add half of the asparagus and cook on high heat for 3 minutes without stirring (you want the asparagus to char). Season with salt and continue cooking for 1 to 2 minutes. Transfer to a dish and set aside. Repeat for the remaining asparagus. Top each mound of salad with some asparagus.

Put each chicken breast between 2 large sheets of parchment paper and pound until flattened. Rub each chicken breast with olive oil and season with salt and pepper. To cook, heat a stovetop grill pan, add the chicken, and cook for 2 to 3 minutes on each side until cooked through.

Put the chicken on top of the asparagus and top it with a slice of Gorgonzola. Sprinkle the hazelnuts and a spoonful of dressing over each serving, add a grinding of pepper, and serve.

spicy-crust roasted rack of lamb

3 tablespoons cumin seeds

2 tablespoons coriander seeds

2 teaspoons black peppercorns

4 cloves

4 small dried chiles

2 tablespoons sea salt

grated zest and freshly squeezed juice of 2 unwaxed lemons

¼ cup olive oil

3 racks of lamb, 6 chops each

¾ cup red wine

Mashed Minty Potatoes and Peas, to serve (see below)

serves 8

Heat a dry skillet and add the cumin and coriander seeds, peppercorns, cloves, and chiles. Cook for 1 minute, stirring frequently. Transfer to a mortar and crush coarsely with a pestle. Put in a bowl and stir in the salt, lemon zest and juice, and oil.

Put the racks of lamb into a large roasting pan. Rub the spice mixture into the lamb, smearing well all over. Cover and chill in the refrigerator overnight.

Cook the lamb in a preheated oven at 400°F for 20 minutes then reduce the oven temperature to 350°F. Cook for a further 20 minutes for rare lamb, 25 minutes for medium, and 35 minutes for well done. Remove from the oven, transfer to a carving board, and let rest for 5 minutes in a warm place.

Meanwhile, add the wine and ¾ cup water to the roasting pan and set it on top of the stove over high heat. Stir to scrape up all the roasted bits on the bottom of the pan, and boil until reduced by half.

Cut the lamb into separate chops and arrange on top of the mashed minty potatoes and peas. Spoon a little sauce over the top and serve.

This simple combination creates a two-in-one vegetable dish, making life in the kitchen a little easier. The mashed potato mixture can be prepared in advance, but don't add the mint until just before serving or it will lose its vibrant, fresh look.

mashed minty potatoes & peas

Cook the potatoes in a large saucepan of boiling, salted water for about 20 minutes, or until tender when pierced with a knife. Drain well and return them to the pan. Shake the pan a few times, then put over low heat for 2 minutes to steam off any excess moisture.

Add the butter, egg, milk, salt, and pepper to the pan. Stir briefly, then remove from the heat and crush the potatoes briefly with the back of a wooden spoon. Keep the potatoes warm while you cook the peas.

Bring a saucepan of salted water to a boil, add the peas, and cook for 2 minutes. Drain well, add to the potatoes, then add the mint. Mix gently, crushing the peas lightly into the potato, but keeping some whole.

3 lb. boiling potatoes, cut into equal pieces

4 tablespoons butter

1 egg, beaten

½ cup milk

10 oz. frozen baby peas, 2 cups

a bunch of mint, chopped

sea salt and freshly ground black pepper

serves 8

A summery way of enjoying roast beef without too much heat from the kitchen. Parboiling the potatoes before roasting means that they won't dry out and shrivel as they roast.

seared peppered beef salad
with horseradish dressing

1 lb. baby new potatoes, unpeeled, parboiled for 12–15 minutes (see box below), until nearly cooked through

2 tablespoons olive oil

8 oz. cherry or grape tomatoes

4 tenderloin steaks, 4 oz. each

1 tablespoon Worcestershire sauce

2 cups arugula

1 cup sugar snap peas, trimmed, blanched, refreshed (see below), and cut in half lengthwise

sea salt and freshly ground black pepper

horseradish dressing

3 tablespoons sour cream or crème fraîche

1–2 tablespoons creamed horseradish

a squeeze of fresh lemon juice

a stovetop grill pan

serves 4

Put the parboiled potatoes in a roasting pan and toss with 1 tablespoon oil, to coat. Sprinkle with salt and black pepper, transfer to a preheated oven at 425°F, and roast for 25 to 30 minutes until browned and starting to crisp.

Remove from the oven and, using a large metal spoon, push the potatoes to one end of the pan, in a pile. Put the tomatoes into the empty half of the pan and sprinkle with 1 tablespoon olive oil, salt, and pepper. Roast in the oven for 15 minutes until just soft.

Meanwhile, put all the dressing ingredients in a bowl and mix well. Add salt and pepper to taste.

Sprinkle the steaks with plenty of black pepper and drizzle with the Worcestershire sauce. Preheat a stovetop grill pan, add the beef, and sear for 1 to 2 minutes on each side or until cooked to your liking. Set aside to rest.

Put the arugula and the sugar snap peas in a bowl and toss well. Divide between 4 serving plates. Spoon the potatoes and tomatoes around the arugula and peas.

Slice the beef fillet diagonally and arrange the slices over the salad. Top with a spoonful of horseradish dressing and serve immediately, with any remaining dressing served separately.

Blanching, refreshing, and parboiling

- *"Blanching" means partially cooking foods, especially vegetables, by dunking them briefly in boiling water. This is especially good for green beans and broccoli, when you want a good, crunchy salad or if you are going to stir-fry the vegetables afterwards. Drain as soon as they turn a bright green, then refresh (see below).*

- *"Refreshing" is when the blanched food is plunged into ice water to stop it cooking and to set the color. Drain again when it's cold.*

- *"Parboiling" is when the foods, often vegetables, are half cooked by boiling in order to be finished by some other cooking method, often roasting. Parboiling potatoes and parsnips before roasting them stops them drying out or shriveling before they are roasted and cooked through.*

For added luxury, use a mixture of porcini and portobello mushrooms. Just make sure they are completely cold when you put them onto the dough, and drain off any excess liquid.

beef en croûte

4 tablespoons olive oil

3 shallots, finely chopped

2 garlic cloves, chopped

6 oz. portobello mushrooms, sliced

3½ lb. beef tenderloin, trimmed

1 lb. puff or shortcrust pastry dough

2 eggs, beaten

sea salt and freshly ground black pepper

Mustard Sauce, to serve (see below)

a baking sheet, lightly oiled

serves 8

Put 2 tablespoons of the oil in a skillet, heat gently, then add the shallots, garlic, and mushrooms. Cook for 15 minutes, stirring frequently, until soft but not browned and all the liquid has evaporated. Season with salt and pepper, let cool, then chill in the refrigerator.

Put 1 tablespoon of the oil in a roasting pan and put in a preheated oven at 425°F for 5 minutes. Rub the tenderloin all over with the remaining oil and salt and pepper, and transfer to the preheated roasting pan. Cook for 15 minutes, then remove from the oven. Transfer the beef to a plate, reserving the meat juices for the mustard sauce (below), and let cool until completely cold. (At this stage, you can make the mustard sauce in the roasting pan and reheat it when you need it.)

Roll out the dough to a rectangle large enough to wrap around the beef. Brush lightly with the beaten eggs. Spoon the mushroom mixture evenly over the dough, leaving a 2-inch border all around the edges. Put the cold beef in the middle of the dough, on top of the mushrooms, and either roll the dough around the beef or wrap, as if covering a package. Try not to have too much dough at the ends, and trim to avoid areas of double dough. Turn the package so that the seam is underneath, and transfer to a lightly oiled baking sheet. Brush all over with the beaten eggs and chill for 2 hours.

Cook the beef package on the middle shelf of a preheated oven at 400°F for 20 minutes. Reduce the oven temperature to 350°F and continue cooking for 15 minutes for rare, 35 minutes for medium, and 50 minutes for well done. If you are cooking to well done, you may need to reduce the oven temperature to prevent the dough from burning while the beef cooks through. To serve, cut the beef package into thick slices and serve with the mustard sauce.

mustard sauce

2 tablespoons smooth Dijon mustard

2 tablespoons whole-grain mustard

½ cup white wine

1¾ cups heavy cream

reserved juices from roasting the beef

serves 8

This sauce is rather delicious but also rich, so a little goes a long way.

Put the mustards, white wine, cream, and roasting juices in a saucepan. Bring to a boil, then simmer for 5 minutes. Serve hot with the beef.

FAMILY GATHERINGS

Now that you are married, there will be times when
you will want to entertain your family and your
in-laws—a great opportunity to show off your new china,
glass-, and tableware. Take the stress out of preparing
for these gatherings with this delicious selection of ideas
that are bound to impress. There are suggestions for
summer and winter get-togethers, as well as some
tempting dishes for vegetarian relatives.

roasted vegetable dauphinois

1 garlic clove

butter, softened, for brushing

1 lb. parsnips, cut into
½-inch diagonal slices

a handful of fresh sage leaves

12 oz. carrots, cut into
½-inch diagonal slices

12 oz. uncooked unpeeled
beets, scrubbed well and cut
into ½-inch diagonal slices

1¼ cups heavy cream

1 tablespoon olive oil

sea salt and freshly ground
black pepper

a baking dish, about
12 inches square

serves 4

This rich, creamy, garlicky sauce is offset by the earthy flavors of root vegetables, plus the slightly tart and highly aromatic sage. It is easy to prepare, and non-vegetarians will love it too—it's delicious with lamb. Serve with roasted potatoes and a herby salad with mustard dressing.

Rub the garlic around the base and sides of the baking dish, then brush with butter. Pack overlapping slices of parsnips into the dish. Season well with salt and pepper, then add one-third of the sage leaves.

Repeat the process, first with the carrots, then the beets, seasoning each layer with salt and pepper and dotting with the remaining sage. Pour over the cream.

Cover the dish with foil and bake in a preheated oven at 400°F for 1 hour 40 minutes. Remove the foil and lightly sprinkle the top with the olive oil. Return to the oven and continue cooking for a further 20 minutes or until the vegetables are very tender.

leek, feta, & black olive tart

This tart can be made with a multitude of complementary toppings: onion, thyme, and blue cheese; wild mushroom and goat cheese; or spinach, ricotta, and pine nuts.

Roll out the dough to fit the pan almost exactly. Trim and discard a tiny strip around the edge of the dough so that it will rise evenly.

Heat a wok or skillet, add the oil and leeks, and stir-fry until beginning to soften. Add just a little salt, then stir in the dill. Transfer to a colander to drain. Let cool.

Arrange the leeks over the dough. Top with the feta and olives. Bake in a preheated oven at 400°F for 35 minutes, or until the crust has risen and is golden brown. Serve with a salad of mixed leaves.

13 oz. puff pastry dough
(from 17 oz. box), thawed
if frozen

1 tablespoon olive oil

14 oz. leeks, thinly sliced,
about 2¼ cups

a large handful of fresh dill,
coarsely chopped

8 oz. feta cheese, cut into
small cubes

4 oz. pitted black olives,
about ⅔ cup

sea salt

mixed salad leaves, to serve

a baking pan, about
12 x 8 inches

serves 4–6

This tart is made extra special by blending in a little smoked salmon (you could also use gravlax) at the same time as the eggs and cream. This gives the tart a mysterious, slightly smoky flavor and a velvety texture.

salmon, dill, & parmesan tart
with pickled cucumber

1 recipe Pâte Brisée (see page 182)

salmon and dill filling

1 lb. fresh salmon fillets (with or without skin)

1¼ cups heavy cream

3 oz. smoked salmon pieces (scraps will do, but cut off any brown bits)

3 large eggs, beaten

3 tablespoons chopped fresh dill, plus extra dill sprigs to garnish

1 oz. freshly grated Parmesan cheese (⅓ cup)

sea salt and freshly ground black pepper

cucumber topping

2 large cucumbers

1 tablespoon sea salt

1 tablespoon sugar

½ cup white wine or cider vinegar

2 tablespoons chopped fresh dill

freshly ground white pepper

a tart pan, 10 inches diameter

foil or parchment paper and baking beans

a baking sheet

serves 6–8

Bring the dough to room temperature. Roll it out thinly on a lightly floured work surface, then use to line the tart pan. Chill or freeze for 15 minutes. Line the tart case with foil or parchment paper (flicking the edges inwards toward the center so that they don't catch on the dough), then fill with baking beans. Set on a baking sheet and bake blind in the center of a preheated oven at 400°F for 10 to 12 minutes.

Remove the foil or parchment paper and the baking beans and return the tart case to the oven for a further 5 to 7 minutes to dry out completely. Remove from the oven and reduce the oven temperature to 375°F.

Put the salmon fillets in a shallow saucepan and cover them with cold water. Add a little salt and bring slowly to a boil. Just before the water boils, turn off the heat and leave the salmon in the water until it is cold—by then it will be cooked and very moist. Lift it out of the water and drain well. Peel off any skin and check for any bones. Flake coarsely.

Put the cream in a blender, add the smoked salmon and eggs, then blend until smooth. Season well with salt and pepper and stir in the dill. Sprinkle the salmon flakes over the base of the tart and pour in the smoked salmon and cream mixture. Sprinkle with the Parmesan, set on a baking sheet, and bake in the preheated oven for 25 minutes, until just set. Remove from the oven and let cool completely.

Meanwhile, to make the cucumber topping, peel the cucumbers, then slice them as thinly as possible using a mandoline or a food processor. Spread in a colander and sprinkle with the salt, mixing well. Stand the colander on a plate and leave to drain for 30 minutes. Rinse well and squeeze the excess moisture out of the cucumbers. Spread the cucumbers over a large plate.

Dissolve the sugar in the vinegar and stir in the dill. Pour this over the cucumber and let marinate for at least 1 hour before serving.

To serve, drain the cucumbers well and arrange them casually over the top of the salmon tart. Grind over lots of white pepper, top with the dill sprigs, then serve immediately. Any extra cucumber salad can be served on the side.

Good fishmongers will make sure the thin grey membrane that lies under the skin is removed; but if it isn't, insist that it is, all the way down the tail, because it's a difficult job to do at home.

whole roast monkfish

about 12 thin slices bacon or prosciutto—enough to cover the fish

1 monkfish tail, about 18 oz.

2 tablespoons extra virgin olive oil

1½ cups sliced mushrooms, about 8 oz.

2 large garlic cloves, crushed

1 cup dry white wine

2 lb. vine-ripened tomatoes, peeled (see page 49), seeded, and chopped

2 tablespoons sour cream or crème fraîche

a handful of fresh basil leaves, chopped

coarse sea salt

serves 4

Set the bacon on a work surface with the slices slightly overlapping each other. Put the monkfish on top, belly up. Wrap it in the bacon with the ends overlapping across the belly. Turn it over and set aside.

Heat the oil in a large skillet. Add the mushrooms and a pinch of salt and cook until browned, 3 to 5 minutes. Stir in the garlic, then add the wine, and cook over high heat for 1 minute. Stir in the tomatoes, salt lightly, and simmer gently for 5 minutes.

Pour the tomato sauce into a baking dish just large enough to hold the fish. Set the fish on top and roast in a preheated oven at 425°F for 15 minutes. Lower the oven temperature to 400°F and roast for another 30 minutes. Remove from the oven and transfer the fish to a plate. Stir the sour cream and basil into the tomato sauce. Set the monkfish back on top and serve.

hake in green sauce

12 mussels (to clean them, see note on page 59)

16 clams

½ cup cava sparkling wine

4 hake or whiting steaks cut through the bone, about 8 oz. each (leave the bone in)

⅔ cup olive oil

4 garlic cloves, thinly sliced

1 tablespoon finely chopped fresh flat-leaf parsley

1 tablespoon finely chopped fresh cilantro

sea salt

serves 4

Put the mussels, clams, and wine in a saucepan over high heat. As the shellfish open, remove them to a bowl, and cover with plastic wrap. Discard any that don't open. Pour the cooking juices through a cheesecloth-lined strainer and set aside.

Put the hake on a plate and sprinkle with a little salt 10 minutes before cooking.

Put the oil and garlic in a heavy skillet and heat gently so the garlic turns golden slowly and doesn't burn. Remove the garlic with a slotted spoon and set aside until ready to serve.

Pour two-thirds of the oil into a measuring cup and reserve. Add the hake to the oil left in the pan. Cook over very low heat, moving the pan in a circular motion—keep taking it off the heat so it doesn't cook too quickly (the idea is to encourage the oozing of the juices instead of letting them sauté and burn). Add the reserved oil bit by bit as you move the pan, so an emulsion starts to form. When all the oil has been added, remove the fish to a plate and keep it warm. Put the pan on the heat, add the reserved clam juices, and stir to form the sauce.

Return the fish to the pan, add the chopped parsley and cilantro, and continue to cook until the fish is done, about 5 minutes. Just before serving, add the opened mussels, clams, and fried garlic to heat through. Serve.

Basting the chicken a few times as it cooks will help to keep it moist. To do so, remove the chicken from the oven every 30 minutes or so and spoon the wine juices over the top. Don't over-baste or you will lower the oven temperature and the estimated cooking time will be altered.

whole roasted chicken
with prunes & thyme

1 chicken, about 4 lb.
4 red onions, peeled and cut into 6 wedges
1½ cups pitted prunes
2¾ cups red wine
1 teaspoon sugar
a bunch of thyme sprigs
2 tablespoons butter
sea salt and freshly ground black pepper

kitchen string

serves 4

Loosely tie the legs of the chicken together with twine to keep its plump shape while cooking. Sprinkle with salt and pepper and put it in a large roasting pan. Put the onions and prunes around the chicken and pour the wine over the top. Sprinkle with the sugar and thyme sprigs, then dot the butter over the chicken.

Roast the chicken in a preheated oven at 400°F for about 1½ hours, basting frequently, until the chicken is dark golden brown and cooked all the way through. To test for doneness, use a small knife or skewer to pierce the thickest part of the leg through to the bone—it is cooked when the juices that run out are clear and there is no trace of pink.

Remove the chicken to a board, carve, and serve with the onions and prunes.

You can roast potatoes in other oils, such as canola, or even in lard, but olive oil is much the healthiest, and delicious with it. The sprinkled flour gives the perfect coating to make the outsides crisp. If you don't have rock salt, which adds an extra crunch, use sea salt instead.

roasted potatoes

2 lb. potatoes, cut into 2-inch pieces
⅔ cup olive oil
2 tablespoons butter
1 tablespoon all-purpose flour, seasoned with rock salt and freshly ground black pepper

serves 4

Put the potatoes in a large saucepan, cover with cold water, salt lightly, then bring to a boil. Reduce the heat and simmer for 8 minutes to parboil.

Meanwhile, pour the olive oil into a roasting pan and add the butter. Put in a preheated oven at 425°F for 5 minutes, until smoking hot. Drain the potatoes well and return them to the saucepan. Holding the lid on, shake the pan well to roughen the surface of the potatoes.

Remove the roasting pan from the oven, add the potatoes, and turn them over with a large metal spoon to coat them all over with oil. Sprinkle with the flour, then roast for 45 to 50 minutes until crisp and golden. Use a large, metal spoon to push the potatoes around the pan from time to time during cooking, to prevent them from sticking.

This makes the perfect dish to serve for a long Sunday family lunch. Start with apéritifs and nibbles, then serve this with boiled baby new potatoes and a good red wine. Follow with a cheese platter. An apple tart (see page 152) before coffee makes the perfect ending.

spring lamb stew *with vegetables*

Heat the oil in a large casserole, add the lamb, and brown on all sides, in batches if necessary. When all the lamb has been browned, return it all to the pan, lower the heat slightly, and stir in a pinch of salt and the flour. Cook, stirring to coat evenly, for 1 minute.

Add the tomatoes and garlic to the pan, then stir in the broth, bay leaf, and thyme. Bring to a boil and skim off any foam that rises to the surface. Reduce the heat, then cover and simmer gently for 40 minutes.

Add the carrots, leeks, and turnips and cook for 25 minutes more. Taste and adjust the seasoning with salt and pepper.

Add the peas and cook for 7 minutes. Sprinkle with the parsley and serve immediately.

1 tablespoon safflower oil

1½ lb. boneless rib lamb chops, cubed

1 lb. boneless loin lamb chops, each one cut into several pieces

1 tablespoon all-purpose flour

2 vine-ripened tomatoes, peeled (see page 49), seeded, and chopped

2 garlic cloves, crushed

2¾ cups lamb or chicken broth

1 fresh bay leaf

a sprig of thyme

4 baby carrots, cut into 1-inch pieces

8 oz. baby leeks, cut into 2-inch lengths

8 oz. baby turnips

8 oz. sugar snap peas

a handful of fresh flat-leaf parsley, chopped

coarse sea salt and freshly ground black pepper

serves 4

---

4 thick-cut pork chops

extra virgin olive oil

coarse sea salt and freshly ground black pepper

mustard and vinegar sauce

¼ cup wine, dry white or red

1 cup fresh chicken broth

¼ cup tarragon or sherry vinegar

4 tablespoons unsalted butter

3 shallots, finely chopped

1 tablespoon all-purpose flour

2 teaspoons tomato paste

1 teaspoon coarse Dijon mustard

8 French cornichons, sliced

a sprig of fresh tarragon, leaves stripped and chopped

a small handful of fresh flat-leaf parsley, chopped

a stovetop grill pan

serves 2-4

pork chops *with piquant sauce*

To make the sauce, put the wine and stock in a small saucepan. Bring to a boil for 1 minute, then stir in the vinegar. Set aside.

Melt the butter in another saucepan. Add the shallots and cook until soft, 3 to 5 minutes. Add the flour and cook, stirring, for 1 minute. Add the warm broth mixture and tomato purée and mix well. Simmer gently for 15 minutes.

Meanwhile, to cook the pork chops, rub a ridged stovetop grill pan with the oil and heat on high. When hot, add the pork chops and cook for 4 to 5 minutes. Turn and cook the other side for 3 to 4 minutes. Remove from the heat and season the chops on both sides with salt and pepper.

Stir the mustard, cornichons, tarragon, and parsley into the sauce and serve immediately, with the pork chops.

Only the very best meat should be used for this classic English Sunday dinner, and you are in the hands of your butcher for that, so choose well! The art is not so much in the cooking as in the timing, so you don't end up with everybody waiting at the table, while you have forgotten to make the gravy or put the Yorkshire pudding in early enough. This timetable, for serving a roast at 1:00 pm, assumes 6½ lb. beef on the bone, which will take about 1 hour 40 minutes plus 20 minutes resting time—2 hours in all.

roast beef *with all the trimmings*

6½ lb bone-in beef rib roast (2–3 bones)

2 tablespoons all-purpose flour

1 tablespoon hot dry mustard powder

3 oz. beef dripping, shortening, or ¼ cup olive oil

3 onions, quartered

8–10 potatoes, cut into chunks and parboiled (see page 103)

5–6 parsnips, cut in half lengthwise

sea salt and freshly ground black pepper

accompaniments

1 recipe Horseradish Sauce (see page 181)

1 recipe Yorkshire Pudding (see page 185)

about 3 lb. green vegetable, such as cabbage, sliced and steamed or boiled

1 recipe Gravy (see page 178)

an instant-read thermometer

serves 8–10

10:45 Preheat the oven to 475°F. Season the meat with salt and pepper, mix the flour and the mustard powder, and pat it onto the beef fat. Put the dripping or oil in the roasting pan, put the onions in the middle, and set the beef, fat side up, on top.

11:00 Put the potatoes and parsnips around the meat and put the pan in the oven.

11:10 Make the horseradish sauce as directed on page 181 and set aside.

11:20 Reduce oven temperature to 375°F, baste the beef, and turn the vegetables in the fat.

11:40 Baste the beef and turn the potatoes and parsnips in the fat.

12:10 Repeat.

12:29 Increase the oven temperature to 475°F and spoon ¼ cup of the fat into the large Yorkshire pudding pan, if using.

12:30 Heat the fat on the top of the stove and pour the Yorkshire pudding batter into the pan, or wait to do this until 12:42 if you are making individual Yorkshire puddings (see below)

12:31 Put the Yorkshire pudding pan in the oven.

12:33 Put the green vegetable on to boil. Insert a meat thermometer into the beef.

12:40 Take the beef out now, or when the thermometer registers 175°F (or a little below if you like beef very rare). Lift the beef onto a serving dish, add the vegetables, and set aside in a warm place. It will go on cooking as it rests.

12:42 Spoon off the fat and retain it for another time, or spoon into the small Yorkshire pudding pans, pour in the batter, then put in the oven.

12:45 Make the gravy in the roasting pan and pour into a gravy boat.

12:50 Dish up the green vegetable and keep it warm.

12:58 Serve the Yorkshire pudding around the beef or on a separate platter.

1:00 Put the beef on the table with the horseradish sauce and the gravy.

butternut squash
with pistou

Butternut and pistou aren't obvious partners, but the sweetness of squash goes very well with the garlicky basil sauce. This is best served with roast lamb or chicken because the pistou makes a lovely sauce for it all.

⅓ cup extra virgin olive oil
4 garlic cloves
a large handful of fresh basil leaves
2 butternut squash, about 1½ lb. each
fine sea salt

serves 4

To make the pistou, put the oil, garlic, basil leaves, and a pinch of salt in a small food processor. Blend well. Transfer to a small bowl. Alternatively, to prepare without a machine, crush the garlic, chop the basil leaves, then mix with the oil and salt.

Trim the stem from the squash and cut in half lengthwise. Scoop out the seeds. Arrange the squash halves in a roasting pan and sprinkle with salt. Brush generously with the pistou, letting it well up a bit in the cavity if you like. Roast in a preheated oven at 400°F until just browned at the edges and tender when pierced with a knife, 40 to 45 minutes. Serve hot, with the remaining pistou.

Which vegetables are good for roasting?

• *All root vegetables are good roasted, such as potatoes, carrots, parsnips, sweet potatoes, and beets.*

• *Most of the onion family—including onions (whole, cut in half or in wedges), shallots, and garlic.*

• *Starchy vegetables like pumpkin and butternut squash.*

• *Fleshy ones like bell peppers, zucchini, and eggplant.*

---

savoy cabbage
with bacon & cream

Based loosely on a traditional French dish that includes pheasant, this recipe is a very elegant way to dress up a rustic vegetable. It goes best with poultry and potatoes, both roasted.

1 bay leaf
1 Savoy cabbage, about 3 lb.
2 tablespoons unsalted butter
1 tablespoon extra virgin olive oil
4 oz. thinly sliced pancetta, chopped
a sprig of fresh sage, leaves stripped and thinly sliced
¼ cup sour cream, crème fraîche, or heavy cream
sea salt and freshly ground black pepper

serves 4

Bring a large saucepan of water to a boil with the bay leaf and a large pinch of salt. Quarter the cabbage and blanch in the boiling water for 2 to 3 minutes. Drain well.

Core the cabbage quarters, then slice crosswise.

Heat the butter and oil in a large skillet. Add the pancetta and sage and cook over high heat, stirring often, for 1 minute. Add the cabbage and a pinch of salt and cook, stirring often, for 2 to 3 minutes.

Stir in the cream and cook until warmed through, about 1 minute. Season generously with pepper and mix well. Add salt to taste and serve hot.

Here, thyme and sour cream transform ordinary
boiled carrots into something subtly sumptuous.

carrots *with cream & herbs*

2 lb. baby carrots, trimmed,
or medium carrots

3 tablespoons unsalted butter

a sprig of thyme

2 tablespoons sour cream or
crème fraîche

several sprigs of chervil

a small bunch of chives

fine sea salt

serves 4

If using larger carrots, cut them diagonally into 2-inch slices. Put in a large saucepan (the carrots should fit in almost a single layer for even cooking). Add the butter and set over low heat. Cook to melt the butter and coat, about 3 minutes. Half fill the saucepan with water, then add a pinch of salt and the thyme. Cover and cook until the water is almost completely evaporated, 10 to 20 minutes.

Stir in the cream and add salt to taste. Using kitchen shears, snip the chervil and chives over the top, mix well, and serve.

Variation In spring, when turnips are sweet, they make a nice addition to this dish. Peel and quarter large turnips, or just peel baby ones—the main thing is to ensure that all the vegetable pieces (carrot and turnip) are about the same size so that they cook evenly. Halve the carrot quantity and complete with turnips, or double the recipe. Sprinkle with a large handful of just-cooked shelled peas before serving for extra crunch and pretty color.

French beans are the classic accompaniment for lamb,
but they are equally delicious with fish and chicken.

french beans *with garlic*

Bring a large saucepan of water to the boil. Add the beans and cook for 3 to 4 minutes from the time the water returns to the boil. Drain and refresh under cold running water. Set aside.

Heat the oil and butter in a skillet. Add the garlic, beans, and salt, and cook over high heat for 1 minute, stirring. Remove from the heat and stir in the parsley and lemon juice, if using. Sprinkle with pepper and serve.

Variation For mixed beans, halve the quantity of green beans and add a 15-oz. can of drained French flageolet beans to the cooked green beans when sautéing with the garlic. Instead of lemon juice, stir in 3 to 4 tablespoons sour cream or crème fraîche just before serving.

1½ lb. small thin green beans

2 tablespoons extra virgin olive oil

1 tablespoon unsalted butter

2 garlic cloves, crushed

a handful of fresh flat-leaf
parsley, chopped

1 teaspoon freshly squeezed
lemon juice (optional)

coarse sea salt and freshly
ground black pepper

serves 4

EASY ENTERTAINING

*One of the greatest joys of cooking is entertaining
friends. There is something very satisfying about getting
a group of people around your table and preparing good
food for everyone to share. When you invite friends to
dinner, you won't want to spend all evening in the
kitchen, missing out on the fun. So these recipes are
quick to prepare, or can be prepared ahead of time,
so you, too, can enjoy the company as much as the food.*

onion tart

Every good cook should be able to make a savory tart, and this has to be one of the most delicious and popular. As it bakes, it fills your home with gorgeous baking aromas—your guests will be impressed.

1⅔ cups all-purpose flour, plus extra for dusting

1¾ sticks cold butter, cut into small pieces

2 eggs, beaten

filling

6 tablespoons butter

2 tablespoons olive oil

1 lb. onions, thinly sliced

2 eggs

½ cup light cream

sea salt and freshly ground black pepper

a tart pan, 8 inches diameter

parchment paper and baking beans or uncooked rice

serves 4

Sift the flour into a bowl and add the butter. Using your fingertips, rub the butter into the flour until the mixture looks like fine bread crumbs. Add the beaten eggs and, using a round-bladed knife, cut through the mixture until it forms a ball. Knead lightly in the bowl with floured hands until evenly mixed, then cover and chill in the refrigerator for 20 minutes.

Roll out the dough on a lightly floured surface to a circle at least 2 inches bigger in diameter than the base of the tart pan. Drape the dough over the rolling pin, carefully lift it up, and lay it over the top of the pan. Gently press the dough into the pan, making sure there are no air pockets, then use a sharp knife to trim off the excess dough. Chill the pie crust in the refrigerator for 20 minutes.

To make the filling, heat the butter and oil in a saucepan, add the onions, and cook over low heat for 30 minutes until soft and translucent, but not brown.

Line the pie crust dough with parchment paper and baking beans or rice and bake in a preheated oven at 400°F for 20 minutes. Remove the baking beans or rice and parchment, reduce to 325°F and cook for a further 15 minutes until the crust is set and lightly golden.

Put the eggs and cream in a large bowl and beat until mixed. Add the onions with salt and pepper to taste. Pour into the pie crust and bake in the oven for 25 minutes until set and golden. Serve warm or cold with tomato salsa.

tomato salsa

4 vine-ripened tomatoes, peeled (see page 49)

3 scallions, chopped

freshly squeezed juice of 1 lemon

a bunch of fresh flat-leaf parsley, chopped

sea salt and freshly ground black pepper

serves 4

Cut each tomato into quarters, remove the core and seeds, and chop the flesh. Put in a bowl and add the scallions, lemon juice, parsley, and salt and pepper, to taste. Mix well, then set aside for 2 hours to let the flavors develop. Serve with the onion tart.

A comforting bowl of risotto is always a welcome treat for guests, and this version is particularly creamy and satisfying. Gorgonzola is a strong Italian cheese with blue-green marbling that works well alongside the cool ricotta in this recipe.

gorgonzola & ricotta risotto
with crisp sage leaves

about 6 cups hot chicken broth or Vegetable Broth (see page 178)

1 stick unsalted butter

1 onion, finely chopped

2 cups risotto rice

⅓ cup dry white vermouth

1 tablespoon chopped fresh sage leaves

¾ cup Gorgonzola cheese, crumbled

¾ cup fresh ricotta cheese

sea salt and freshly ground black pepper

crisp sage leaves

about 30 fresh sage leaves with stalks

oil, for deep-frying

an electric deep-fryer or wok

serves 4

To make the crisp sage leaves, pat them thoroughly dry with paper towels. Heat the oil to 350°F in a deep-fryer or wok. If using a deep-fryer, put the leaves in the basket and lower into the hot oil. It will hiss alarmingly, but don't worry. Immediately the hissing has stopped, lift the basket out and shake off the excess oil. (If using a wok, use tongs or a slotted spoon to remove the leaves.) Put the leaves on paper towels to drain. Season with a sprinkling of salt and set aside. They will crisp up as they cool.

Put the broth in a saucepan and keep at a gentle simmer. Melt half the butter in a large, heavy saucepan and add the onion. Cook gently for 10 minutes until soft, golden, and translucent but not browned. Add the rice and stir until well coated with the butter and heated through. Pour in the vermouth and boil hard until it has reduced and almost disappeared. This will remove the taste of raw alcohol. Stir in the chopped fresh sage leaves.

Begin adding the broth, a large ladle at a time, stirring gently until each ladle has been almost absorbed by the rice. The risotto should be kept at a bare simmer throughout cooking, so don't let the rice dry out—add more broth as necessary. About halfway through the cooking time, stir in the Gorgonzola until melted. Continue adding broth and cooking until the rice is tender and creamy, but the grains still firm. (This should take 15 to 20 minutes depending on the type of rice used—check the package instructions.) The risotto should be quite loose, but not soupy.

Taste and season well with salt and pepper, then beat in the ricotta and remaining butter. Cover and let rest for a couple of minutes so the risotto can relax. You may like to add a little more hot broth to the risotto just before you serve to loosen it, but don't let it wait around too long or the rice will turn mushy. Serve with the fried sage leaves sprinkled on top.

Spaghettini with clams is typically Italian. Shellfish make
a quick pasta dish special—perfect for entertaining.

baby clam sauce

16 oz. spaghettini, freshly cooked

clam sauce

2 lb. small fresh clams, in their shells

½–⅔ cup olive oil

1 garlic clove, peeled but left whole

½ teaspoon hot red pepper flakes

2 handfuls of fresh parsley,
finely chopped

to serve

freshly ground black pepper

chopped fresh parsley

extra virgin olive oil

serves 4-6

Wash the clams in plenty of running water until not a trace of sand is left. Drain well. Put them in a heavy saucepan over high heat. Cover with a lid and shake the pan until all the clams have opened (remove and discard any that do not open). Strain off the liquid, pour it through a fine sieve, and reserve.

Heat the olive oil in a large saucepan, add the garlic and pepper flakes, and heat through gently. When the garlic starts to turn golden, discard it and the pepper flakes. Add the clams to the pan, together with their strained cooking liquid. Add the parsley and cook gently for 1 to 2 minutes for the flavors to blend.

Add the clams and their sauce to the freshly cooked spaghettini and mix well. Tip onto a large serving plate and top with lots of black pepper, some more parsley, and olive oil. Serve at once.

Variation To make a tomato version of this sauce, peel, seed, and chop 1 lb. plum tomatoes. Add them to the oil at the same time as the garlic and chile. Cook over low heat for 20 to 30 minutes until reduced to a creamy mass. Add the clams and the strained juices and cook for 1 to 2 minutes for the flavors to blend. Add the parsley and proceed as in the main recipe.

24 large uncooked shrimp,
shelled and deveined

¼ cup Chile Oil (see page 181)

freshly squeezed juice of 1 lemon

sea salt and freshly ground black pepper

pistachio and mint pesto

2 oz. shelled pistachios, about ⅓ cup

a bunch of mint leaves

1 garlic clove, crushed

2 scallions, chopped

½ cup extra virgin olive oil

1 tablespoon white wine vinegar

to serve

1 lemon, cut into wedges

crusty bread

serves 4

shrimp *with chile oil & pistachio & mint pesto*

To make the pesto, put the nuts, mint, garlic, and scallions in a food processor and blend coarsely. Add the oil and purée until fairly smooth and bright green. Stir in the vinegar and season to taste with salt and pepper. Set aside while you prepare the shrimp, or store in a screwtop jar in the refrigerator for up to 5 days.

Put the shrimp in a shallow dish and sprinkle with the chile oil, salt, and pepper. Cover and let marinate for at least 30 minutes or longer, if possible.

When ready to serve, thread the shrimp onto skewers and cook on a preheated outdoor grill or stovetop grill pan, or under a hot broiler, for about 2 minutes on each side until charred and tender—the flesh should be just opaque. Do not overcook the shrimp or they will be tough.

Transfer to separate plates or a large platter. Sprinkle with the lemon juice and serve with the pesto, lemon wedges, and crusty bread to mop up the juices.

seared swordfish
with avocado & salsa

Put the oil, lime zest, and juice in a small bowl and beat well. Add plenty of black pepper. Put the swordfish steaks in a shallow dish and pour over the oil and lime mixture, making sure the fish is coated on both sides. Cover and refrigerate for up to 1 hour.

Meanwhile, to make the salsa, put the onion, chile, tomato, oil, lime zest, and juice in a bowl. Mix gently, then cover and refrigerate.

Heat a grill or stovetop grill pan until hot, add the fish, and cook for 2 to 3 minutes on each side or until just cooked through. Transfer the swordfish to 4 serving plates. Divide the avocado slices between the 4 plates, spoon over the salsa, sprinkle with cilantro, and serve with lime wedges.

2 tablespoons olive oil

grated zest and juice of 2 unwaxed limes

4 swordfish steaks

2 large, just-ripe avocados, cut in half, pitted, peeled, and sliced

freshly ground black pepper

salsa

1 small red onion, chopped

1 red chile, seeded and finely chopped

1 large ripe tomato, cut in half, seeded, and chopped

3 tablespoons extra virgin olive oil

grated zest and juice of 1 unwaxed lime

to serve

a bunch of cilantro, chopped

1 lime, cut into wedges

a stovetop grill pan (optional)

serves 4

peppered tuna steak *with salsa rossa*

Salsa rossa is one of those divine Italian sauces that transforms simple meat and fish dishes into food nirvana. The slight sweetness from the bell peppers is a good foil for the spicy pepper crust.

To make the salsa rossa, broil the pepper until charred all over, then put it in a plastic bag and let cool. Remove and discard the skin and seeds, reserving any juices. Chop the flesh coarsely.

Heat the oil gently in a skillet, then add the garlic and sauté for 3 minutes. Add the tomatoes, pepper flakes, and oregano and simmer gently for 15 minutes. Stir in the chopped pepper and the vinegar and simmer for a further 5 minutes to evaporate any excess liquid. Transfer to a blender and purée until fairly smooth. Add salt and pepper to taste and let cool. It may be stored in a screwtop jar in the refrigerator for up to 3 days.

Put the crushed peppercorns on a large plate. Brush the tuna steaks with oil, then press the crushed peppercorns into both sides of the tuna. Preheat a stovetop grill pan or outdoor grill until hot, add the tuna, and cook for 1 minute on each side. Wrap the tuna loosely in foil and let rest for 5 minutes before serving with the salsa rossa and a salad of mixed leaves.

⅓ cup mixed peppercorns, coarsely crushed

6 tuna steaks, 8 oz. each

1 tablespoon extra virgin olive oil

mixed salad leaves, to serve

salsa rossa

1 large red bell pepper

1 tablespoon extra virgin olive oil

2 garlic cloves, crushed

2 large ripe tomatoes, skinned (see page 49) and coarsely chopped

a small pinch of hot red pepper flakes

1 tablespoon dried oregano

1 tablespoon red wine vinegar

sea salt and freshly ground black pepper

a stovetop grill pan (optional)

serves 6

Baked chicken, swimming in this lemony, spicy marinade makes easy
entertaining. Thighs are the best choice, because they stay tender and
moist, though you could use a whole chicken cut into pieces.

lemon-spiced chicken

8–16 chicken pieces, preferably
thighs (allow 2–4 per person)

1/3 cup extra virgin olive oil

freshly squeezed juice of 2 lemons

1 tablespoon ground cumin

1 teaspoon sweet smoked
Spanish paprika

1/2 teaspoon hot red pepper flakes

1 teaspoon dried oregano

a small bunch of thyme sprigs,
fresh or dried

2 teaspoons coarse sea salt

1 teaspoon coarsely ground
black pepper

Bulghur Wheat Pilaf, to serve
(see below), optional

a baking dish

serves 4

Trim any excess fat from the chicken pieces. Put the chicken
in a baking dish large enough to hold them comfortably (or
divide between 2 dishes). Put the oil, lemon juice, cumin,
paprika, red pepper flakes, oregano, thyme, salt, and pepper
in a bowl and mix well. Pour over the chicken and turn to
coat well. Cover and set aside for at least 30 minutes, or
refrigerate for 6 to 8 hours.

Make sure all the chicken pieces are skin side up in the dish
and roast in a preheated oven at 400°F until browned and
cooked through, 50 to 60 minutes. Serve immediately with
the pan juices poured over, and accompanied by the bulghur
wheat pilaf, if liked.

This is intended as an accompaniment, but if you add some
chopped peppers, mushrooms, cooked peas, wilted spinach,
or crumbled feta, you could serve it as a light meal.

bulghur wheat pilaf

2 tablespoons extra virgin olive oil

a handful of vermicelli or
cappellini, about 1 1/2 oz.

1 1/4 cups bulghur wheat

2 3/4 cups unsalted fresh chicken or
Vegetable Broth (see page 178)

a few sprigs of thyme

sea salt and freshly ground
black pepper

serves 4

Heat the oil in a saucepan, break the vermicelli or cappellini
into small pieces as you add them to the pan, and cook, stirring
regularly until browned, about 5 minutes. Stir in the bulghur
wheat and a good pinch of salt and mix to coat the grains.

Add the stock and thyme, stir, and bring to a boil. Cover,
lower the heat, and cook, undisturbed, until all the liquid has
been absorbed, 10 to 15 minutes.

Fluff up the grains and serve hot.

Braising is a fantastic way to cook thick pork chops, because it makes the meat so tender. Chicken pieces would work equally well. The flavors in this dish point straight to Spain, though it is not traditional. This recipe cries out for advance preparation—the orange, chile, and everything else need time to mingle and develop the flavors—which makes it ideal for entertaining. It's very homey sort of food and perfect with potatoes, preferably fried or mashed. Serve it with a good bottle of Rioja wine.

braised pork chops
with tomato, orange, & chile

3 tablespoons extra virgin olive oil

8 bone-in pork chops, about 8 oz. each, trimmed of fat

3 celery stalks, chopped

1 onion, chopped

4 garlic cloves, finely chopped

½–1 teaspoon hot red pepper flakes

½ cup red wine, preferably Rioja

14 oz. canned chopped tomatoes

freshly squeezed juice of 1 orange, orange shell reserved

1 bay leaf

a few sprigs of fresh oregano or thyme

a handful of fresh flat-leaf parsley leaves, coarsely chopped

sea salt

to serve

Classic Creamy Mashed Potatoes (see page 88)

sugar snap peas, steamed

serves 8

Heat 2 tablespoons of the oil in a large sauté pan with a lid. Add the pork chops and cook until browned, 3 to 5 minutes. Turn and cook the other side (work in batches if they don't all fit in the pan). Transfer to a plate, season with salt, and set aside.

Add the celery and onion to the pan and cook over high heat until browned, 2 to 3 minutes. Add the garlic and red pepper flakes and cook for 30 seconds more. Add the wine and stir, scraping any bits that stick to the bottom of the pan. Boil for 1 minute, then stir in the tomatoes, orange juice, bay leaf, oregano or thyme, and salt, to taste. Quarter the orange used for the juice and put 1 piece in the sauce.

Return the meat to the pan and bury it under the sauce as much as possible. Cover, lower the heat, and simmer gently until tender, about 1 hour. Turn the meat halfway through cooking.

Remove the meat from the sauce, put it on a heatproof plate, and keep warm in a low oven. Raise the heat under the tomato sauce and cook for 3 to 5 minutes to thicken slightly. Remove and discard the orange piece, bay leaf, and herb sprigs. Pile the sauce on top of the pork chops, sprinkle with chopped parsley and serve with mashed potatoes and steamed sugar snap peas.

The best stews are those that are marinated for 24 hours, then cooked slowly for a long time. Unfortunately, they require a lot of advance planning. That is where this recipe comes in handy; it's a sort of cross between beef stew and ragù sauce, without the forward thinking.

beef provençal

1 bay leaf

a few sprigs of thyme

1 small inner celery stalk, with the leaves

2 tablespoons extra virgin olive oil

1 large onion, chopped

2 lb. braising beef, such as chuck, cut into 1½-inch cubes

1 piece of cured ham, preferably a fatty end piece, about 6 oz.

6 garlic cloves, sliced

1 cup dry white or red wine

14 oz. canned chopped tomatoes

⅓ cup pitted black olives

a handful of fresh basil leaves, chopped

sea salt

32 oz. pasta, freshly cooked, to serve

kitchen twine

serves 6

Tie the bay leaf, thyme, and celery stalk together with kitchen twine.

Heat the oil in a large skillet. Add the onion and cook until softened, 2 to 3 minutes. Add the beef, ham, and garlic and cook for 1 to 2 minutes. Season with salt.

Add the wine, boil for 1 minute, then add the tomatoes and the tied bunch of herbs. Cover, lower the heat, and simmer gently until the meat is very tender, about 2 hours.

To serve, remove the bunch of herbs and stir in the olives. The ham can either be shredded and added back to the stew, or simply removed; taste the ham to see which you prefer—sometimes the heel of a cured ham can be quite strong in flavor. Sprinkle with the basil leaves and serve over freshly cooked pasta.

4 rib-eye steaks, about 8 oz. each

2 tablespoons extra virgin olive oil

sea salt and freshly ground black pepper

horseradish and chive butter

1¼ sticks unsalted butter, softened

1½ tablespoons grated fresh horseradish

1 tablespoon chopped fresh chives

to serve (optional)

sautéed potatoes

green salad

serves 4

pan-fried steak
with horseradish & chive butter

To make the horseradish and chive butter, put the butter, horseradish, and chives in a bowl and beat well. Season to taste with salt and pepper. Form into a log shape, wrap in foil, and chill in the refrigerator for about 30 minutes.

Season the steaks with salt and pepper. Heat the oil in a skillet until very hot and sauté the steaks over medium-high heat for 3 minutes on each side for rare, a couple of minutes longer for medium.

Top each steak with 2 slices of the horseradish butter and set aside to rest in a warm oven for 5 minutes. Serve with sautéed potatoes and a green salad, if liked.

DESSERTS

Whether it's something sweet to make a mid-week dinner special or something decadent to round off a family gathering, you will find lots of inspiration here. From fruity desserts for summer such as Apricot and Orange Gelato (see page 143) to warming winter ideas such as Rice Pudding (see page 151), there is something here for every season and every occasion.

apricot & orange gelato

8 oz. dried apricots,
1¼ cups, chopped

¾ cup plus 2 tablespoons sugar

2 teaspoons freshly grated
orange zest and 1 cup freshly
squeezed orange juice,
2–3 unwaxed oranges

3 tablespoons freshly squeezed
lemon juice, about 1 medium lemon

1 teaspoon orange-flower water

2 tablespoon Cointreau
(or other citrus liqueur)

8 oz. mascarpone cheese, in pieces

1¾ cups light cream

8–12 cookies or sliced brioche,
to serve (optional)

*an electric ice cream maker or
a 6-cup freezerproof container
with a lid*

serves 4-6

Put the chopped apricots in a saucepan and cover with boiling water by about 1 inch. Return to a boil, reduce the heat, and simmer for 10 minutes. Remove from the heat and let stand for 5 minutes.

Put the apricots and their cooking water in a blender (for smooth texture) or food processor (for coarse texture), then add the sugar, orange zest and juice, lemon juice, orange-flower water, and liqueur. Blend well. Add the mascarpone pieces. Blend . Pour out half into a large bowl and set aside.

Add the cream to the machine and blend very briefly until incorporated. Pour this into the bowl with the other mixture and stir well. Let cool, if necessary, over ice water.

Transfer the mixture to an ice cream maker and churn for 20 to 35 minutes or until thick. Spoon into a freezerproof container, cover, and freeze until time to use. Alternatively, freeze the mixture in the container, covered, for 6 hours, beating it once, after 3 hours. Serve in scoops or slices with cookies or cake, if using.

Note When sharply flavored fresh apricots are in season, halve, pit, and broil or bake 1 lb. (8–12 fruit) until they are collapsed, golden, and tender. Use these in place of the dried apricots: they need no further cooking.

bitter chocolate & hazelnut gelato

½ cup blanched (peeled) hazelnuts,
finely chopped

1 cup vanilla sugar or sugar

⅔ cup whole milk

8 oz. bittersweet chocolate,
broken in pieces

1 tablespoon corn syrup

1 tablespoon chocolate or
hazelnut liqueur or dark rum

1¾ cups heavy cream

crisp wafers or cookies, to serve
(optional)

*an electric ice cream maker
or a 1-quart freezerproof container
with a lid*

serves 4-6

Put the chopped hazelnuts in a dry skillet and dry-cook over moderate heat, stirring constantly until they darken and smell toasty, 2 to 3 minutes (take care, because they burn easily). Transfer to a plate and let cool.

Put the toasted hazelnuts and ¼ cup of the sugar in a small electric spice grinder or coffee grinder. Grind in brief bursts, to a smooth, speckly powder.

Put the milk, chocolate, and remaining sugar in a saucepan over very gentle heat. Cook, stirring constantly, until the chocolate melts, then add the corn syrup and ground sugar and nuts. Remove from the heat, put the pan in a bowl of ice water, and let cool. Stir in the liqueur and cream and cool again.

Pour the prepared mixture into the ice cream maker and churn for 20 to 25 minutes or until set. Alternatively, freeze in the container, covered, for 6 hours, beating it once, after 3 hours. Serve in scoops with wafers or cookies, if using.

This amazingly popular dessert actually benefits from being made the day before. For added texture, grind real chocolate in a blender to use for layering and sprinkling.

tiramisù

6 oz. bittersweet chocolate
1¼ cups heavy cream
½ cup Italian espresso coffee
6 tablespoons Marsala wine
8 oz. mascarpone cheese (1 cup)
⅓ cup sugar
2 tablespoons dark rum
2 egg yolks
24 savoiardi or ladyfingers
1 pint fresh raspberries,
plus extra to serve

a serving dish or 4 glasses

serves 4 generously

Put the chocolate in a blender or food processor and grind to a powder. Set aside. Pour the cream into a bowl and whisk until soft peaks form. Set aside.

Pour the espresso into a second bowl and stir in 2 tablespoons of the Marsala. Set aside. Put the mascarpone in a third bowl and whisk in 3 tablespoons of the sugar, then beat in 2 tablespoons of the Marsala and the rum. Set aside.

To make the zabaglione mixture, put the egg yolks, 2 tablespoons Marsala, and the remaining 2 tablespoons sugar in a medium heatproof bowl and beat with a hand-held electric mixer or whisk until well blended. Set over a saucepan of gently simmering water—the bottom of the bowl should at no time be in contact with the water, and do not let the water boil. Whisk the mixture until it is glossy, pale, light, and fluffy and holds a trail when dropped from the whisk. This should take about 5 minutes. Remove from the heat and whisk until cold. Fold in the whipped cream, then fold in the mascarpone mixture.

Dip the savoiardi, one at a time, into the espresso mixture. Do not leave them in for too long or they will disintegrate. Start assembling the tiramisù by arranging half the dipped savoiardi in the bottom of a serving dish or 4 glasses. Trickle over some of the leftover espresso. Add a layer of raspberries.

Sprinkle with one-third of the ground chocolate, then add half the zabaglione-cream-mascarpone mixture. Arrange the remaining savoiardi on top, moisten with any remaining espresso, add some more raspberries and sprinkle with half the remaining chocolate. Finally spoon over the remaining zabaglione-cream-mascarpone and finish with a thick layer of chocolate and extra raspberries. Chill in the refrigerator for at least 3 hours (overnight is better) to let the flavors develop. Serve chilled.

raspberries in champagne gelatin

Put 3 tablespoons hot water in a small heatproof bowl and sprinkle in the gelatin. Set aside in a warm place to dissolve, about 10 minutes. Divide the raspberries between the glasses. Open the champagne and add a little to the dissolved gelatin. Transfer the mixture to a pitcher and add the remaining champagne. Mix gently so that you don't build up a froth. Pour this over the raspberries and chill until set, about 2 hours.

2 envelopes powdered gelatin, ½ oz. each, or 2 tablespoons
1 lb. raspberries, 3 cups
1 bottle champagne, at room temperature

8 glasses

serves 8

Pure indulgence is a crisp meringue with a soft, marshmallow center, filled with whipped cream and topped with berries. Once mastered, you'll discover that a meringue is one of the simplest, prettiest, and most versatile of all desserts. Sharp-flavored fruits, such as raspberries, balance the sweetness of the meringue, though you could use any of your favorite fruits.

raspberry roulade

6 egg whites, at room temperature (see box, below)

a pinch of sea salt

2 cups superfine sugar

2 teaspoons cornstarch

1 teaspoon white wine vinegar

raspberry rose filling

2 cups heavy cream

3–6 tablespoons rose water

2 cups raspberries

a cookie sheet, lined with wax paper

serves 8-10

Put the egg whites and salt in a scrupulously clean, greasefree bowl and, using an electric hand-held mixer, beat until stiff peaks form. (Take care: if there is any trace of egg yolk or grease in the bowl the whites won't whisk properly.)

Sprinkle in 1 tablespoon of sugar at a time and beat between each addition until the meringue is thick and glossy. Add the cornstarch and vinegar and beat until mixed.

Transfer the meringue to the prepared cookie sheet and, using a spatula, spread it into a rectangle about 12 x 16 inches. Smooth the surface. Bake in a preheated oven at 350°F for 17 minutes or until barely crisp. Let cool.

To turn out the meringue, cover with a piece of wax paper, then quickly but carefully invert the cookie sheet onto the work surface. Lift off the cookie sheet, then gently peel off the wax paper from the meringue.

To make the filling, put the cream and rose water in a bowl and beat lightly until soft peaks form. Spoon the cream onto the meringue and spread, leaving a ½-inch border clear all around the edge. Spread the raspberries over the top of the cream.

Lift up the side of the wax paper nearest to you and use it to help roll up the roulade lengthwise. Peel back the paper as you go. Before you reach the end, carefully lift the roulade (still on the paper) onto a platter or board.

Roll the roulade off the paper so that the join is underneath. Slice the dessert into 8 to 10 pieces and serve.

Separating eggs

• *Have 2 bowls ready. Tap the egg on the side of one bowl to crack it in the middle. Using your thumbs, pull open the two halves with the cracked side facing upwards, tipping the yolk into one half and letting any white fall into the bowl. Tip the yolk back and forth between the 2 shell halves until there is no white left around the yolk. Tip the yolk into the other bowl. If any yolk slips into the white, use a shell to scoop it out.*

ricotta cake

⅓ cup plump raisins

¼ cup Cognac

8 oz. ricotta cheese

8 oz. mascarpone cheese

4 large eggs, separated (see page 147)

¼ cup all-purpose flour

grated zest of 1 unwaxed lemon

½ teaspoon ground cinnamon

1 cup sugar

a nonstick cake pan, 9 inches diameter, greased with butter and dusted with flour

serves 4-6

Put the raisins in a small bowl, add the Cognac, and let soak for 15 to 30 minutes.

Put the ricotta, mascarpone, and egg yolks in a mixing bowl and beat until well blended. Add the flour, lemon zest, cinnamon, the pinch of salt, and all but about 1 tablespoon of the sugar. Mix well, then set aside.

Put the egg whites and the remaining sugar in another mixing bowl. Beat with an electric hand mixer on high until stiff peaks form. Transfer one-third of the egg whites to the ricotta mixture and stir to blend. Using a spatula, gently fold in the remaining egg whites, raisins, and Cognac, until no lumps are visible. Pour into the prepared pan.

Bake in a preheated oven at 350°F until browned around the edges and firm, but still jiggly in the middle, 40 to 50 minutes. Let cool completely, then cut into wedges and serve at room temperature.

traditional new york cheesecake

8 oz. graham crackers

1 stick unsalted butter

¼ cup plus 2 tablespoons sugar

filling

1½ sticks unsalted butter

¾ cup sugar

4 extra-large eggs, beaten

3 tablespoons all-purpose flour

finely grated zest and juice of 1 large unwaxed lemon

½ teaspoon vanilla extract

3 packages cream cheese, 8 oz. each, at room temperature

¼ cup milk

topping

1¾ cups sour cream

1 tablespoon confectioners' sugar

freshly squeezed juice of 1 lemon

a springform cake pan, 9 inches diameter, greased

a baking sheet with sides

serves 10-12

To make the crumb base, put the cookies in a large plastic bag and finely crush them with a rolling pin. Melt the butter in a small saucepan over gentle heat, then stir in the crumbs and sugar. Spread the crumb mixture over the base of the prepared cake pan, pressing down lightly. Set the pan on a baking sheet with sides and bake in a preheated oven at 375°F for 8 to 10 minutes. Remove from the oven and let cool. Reduce the oven temperature to 325°F.

To make the filling, put the butter and sugar in a large bowl and, using a wooden spoon or electric hand mixer, beat until pale and fluffy. Gradually beat in the eggs. Mix in the flour, lemon zest, lemon juice, and vanilla. Put the cream cheese in a separate bowl and, using a wooden spoon or electric hand mixer, beat until smooth. Gently beat in the milk, then gradually beat in the butter and sugar mixture. Spoon the mixture onto the crumb base and level the surface. Bake in the preheated oven for 1½ hours.

Meanwhile, to make the topping, put the sour cream, confectioners' sugar, and lemon juice in a large bowl and, using a wooden spoon or electric hand mixer, beat lightly. Cover and chill in the refrigerator until required.

Remove the cheesecake from the oven and increase the temperature to 375°F. Pour the topping over the surface of the cheesecake, level with a spatula, and return to the preheated oven for a further 10 minutes or until set. Turn off the oven, leave the door ajar, and let the cheesecake cool in the oven to prevent it from cracking. Once cool, chill the cheesecake in the refrigerator for 2 hours before serving.

6 peaches, not too ripe

1 tablespoon all-purpose flour

1 tablespoon freshly squeezed lemon juice

3 tablespoons honey

cream or vanilla ice cream, to serve

cobbler topping

½ cup heavy cream

⅓ cup sour cream or crème fraîche

1¼ cups all-purpose flour

¼ cup sugar, plus extra for sprinkling

1 teaspoon baking powder

¼ teaspoon baking soda

a pinch of fine sea salt

4 tablespoons unsalted butter, cut into small pieces

2–3 tablespoons sugar, for sprinkling

a shallow baking dish, 2 quarts

serves 6

Add a basket of blackberries to the peaches, if you like, or use a combination of peaches, apricots, and blackberries.

peach cobbler

Cut the peaches in half, remove the pits, then cut each half into 3 slices. Put them in the baking dish, sprinkle with the flour, and toss well to coat evenly. Add the lemon juice and honey and stir. Set aside.

To make the topping, put the cream and sour cream in a large bowl and stir well. Set aside.

Put the flour, sugar, baking powder, baking soda, and salt in a large bowl and mix well. Add the butter and rub it into the flour with your fingertips until the mixture resembles coarse crumbs. Using a fork, stir in the cream mixture until blended—use your hands at the end if necessary, it should be sticky, thick, and not willing to blend easily.

Drop spoonfuls of the mixture on top of the peaches, leaving gaps to expose the fruit. Sprinkle sugar liberally on top of the batter. Bake in a preheated oven at 375°F until golden, 25 to 35 minutes. Serve warm with cream or ice cream.

rice pudding

½ cup risotto rice, such as arborio

2 cups whole milk, boiled

⅓ cup sugar

1 vanilla bean, split lengthwise with a small sharp knife

1 tablespoon unsalted butter

a pinch of salt

an ovenproof pan with a lid

serves 4

This is a very simple, classic recipe of which there are many versions. Blanching the rice first removes much of the starch, giving a light, delicate result.

Put the rice in a saucepan with a lid and add cold water to cover. Slowly bring to a boil over medium heat, then boil for 5 minutes. Drain the rice and rinse under cold water. Set aside to drain well.

Meanwhile, put the milk in an ovenproof saucepan with a lid and bring to a boil. Add the sugar and vanilla bean. Remove from the heat, cover, and let stand for 15 minutes. Using the tip of the knife, scrape out the vanilla seeds and stir them through the milk.

Add the rice to the milk, then add the butter and salt. Bring slowly to a boil. Cover and transfer to a preheated oven at 350°F. Do not stir. Cook until the rice is tender and the liquid is almost completely absorbed but not dry, 25 to 35 minutes. Serve warm.

apple tart

1 recipe Pâte Brisée (see page 182)

apple filling

4–5 well-flavored eating apples, peeled and cored

3 tablespoons sugar

4 tablespoons unsalted butter, cubed

4–6 tablespoons apricot jam

2 tablespoons Calvados (apple brandy) or brandy

a baking sheet

a false-bottom tart pan, 10 inches diameter

serves 6-8

Bring the dough to room temperature. Preheat the oven to 400°F and put a baking sheet in the oven to heat.

Roll out the dough thinly on a lightly floured work surface and use to line the tart pan. Chill or freeze for 15 minutes.

Meanwhile, slice the apples thinly, and coarsely chop any uneven smaller pieces. Arrange these smaller pieces in the base of the tart. Cover with one-third of the slices any way you like. Arrange the remaining slices neatly in concentric rings over the chopped apples. Sprinkle with the sugar and dot with the butter.

Set the tart pan on the baking sheet and bake in the preheated oven for about 1 hour until the apples are very well browned and the crust golden. Remove from the oven and transfer to a wire rack. Wait for 5 minutes, then remove the tart pan.

Put the apricot jam and Calvados in a small saucepan and warm gently. Strain, then use to glaze the apples. Serve at room temperature.

pumpkin pie

This is the classic American pie. Butternut squash purée makes an acceptable substitute if pumpkin is not available. If you don't want to use canned purée, you can make your own, see note below.

Bring the dough to room temperature. Preheat the oven to 375°F.

Roll out the dough thinly on a lightly floured work surface, then use to line the 2 tart pans or pie plates. Trim and crimp or decorate the edges as you wish. Prick the bases all over with a fork, chill or freeze for 15 minutes, then bake blind following the method given on page 182.

Lower the oven to 325°F.

Put all the filling ingredients in a food processor and blend until smooth. Pour into the pie crusts, set on a baking sheet and bake for about 1 hour or until just set. Remove from the oven and let stand for 10 minutes, then remove the tart pans and let cool for a few minutes. Serve warm or at room temperature, not chilled.

*Note To make the purée, cut a pumpkin or butternut squash into large chunks. Put in a roasting pan and bake in a preheated oven at 325°F for about 1 hour. Scrape the flesh from the skin and purée in a food processor until smooth.

1 recipe American Pie Crust Dough (see page 182)

pumpkin filling

2 cups homemade pumpkin purée* or one 15 oz. can

1/2 cup light brown sugar

3 extra-large eggs

3/4 cup evaporated milk, about 7 oz.

1/2 cup light corn syrup

a good pinch of salt

1 teaspoon ground cinnamon

1/2 teaspoon grated nutmeg

1 teaspoon pure vanilla extract

2 tablespoons rum (optional)

2 tart pans or pie plates, 9 inches diameter

a baking sheet

makes 2 pies, 9 inches diameter

This famous pie hails from the South—it is supposed to look like the thick, dark, muddy waters of the Mississippi Delta. It is very easy to make and perfect for sharing with family and friends.

mississippi mud pie

cookie base

8 oz. graham crackers or digestive biscuits, about 2⅔ cups

4 tablespoons unsalted butter

2 oz. bittersweet chocolate, finely chopped

chocolate filling

6 oz. bittersweet chocolate, chopped

1½ sticks unsalted butter, cut into small pieces

4 extra-large eggs, beaten

½ cup firmly packed light brown sugar

½ cup firmly packed dark brown sugar

1¾ cups heavy cream

chocolate cream

⅔ cup heavy cream, well chilled

3 tablespoons unsweetened cocoa powder

⅓ cup confectioners' sugar

a springform cake pan, 9 inches diameter, well buttered

serves 8

To make the base, put the crackers in a food processor and blend until fine crumbs form. Alternatively, put the crackers in a plastic bag and crush with a rolling pin. Transfer the crumbs to a mixing bowl.

Put the butter and chocolate in a heatproof bowl set over a saucepan of steaming but not boiling water and melt gently (do not let the base of the bowl touch the water). Remove from the heat, stir gently, then stir into the cracker crumbs. When well mixed, transfer the mixture to the prepared pan and, using the back of a spoon, press onto the base and about halfway up the sides of the pan. Chill in the refrigerator while making the filling.

To make the filling, put the chocolate and butter in a heatproof bowl set over a saucepan of steaming but not boiling water and melt gently (do not let the base of the bowl touch the water). Remove from the heat, stir gently, then let cool.

Put the eggs and sugar in a large mixing bowl and, using electric beaters or mixer, beat until thick and foamy. Beat in the cream followed by the melted chocolate. Pour the mixture into the cookie crust and bake in a preheated oven at 350°F for about 45 minutes until just firm. Let cool for a few minutes, then remove from the pan.

To make the chocolate cream, put the cream in a mixing bowl, then sift the cocoa and confectioners' sugar on top and stir gently with a wooden spoon until blended. Cover and chill for 2 hours.

Serve the pie at room temperature with the chocolate cream. The pie can be made up to 2 days in advance and kept, well covered, in the refrigerator. Remove from the refrigerator 30 minutes before serving.

BAKING

Home baking is very rewarding. Not only is the smell so homely and appealing, the results are deliciously tempting. From cakes and cookies to bread, there is nothing quite as enticing as home-baked treats, and you don't need to spend hours in the kitchen to make them. Fresher, tastier, and better for you than store-bought equivalents, there really is no better reason to put on your new apron and get baking.

1⅓ cups self-rising flour

a pinch of salt

a good pinch of baking soda

1 stick unsalted butter, very soft

⅓ cup minus 1 tablespoon sugar

⅓ cup lightly packed light brown sugar

½ teaspoon pure vanilla extract

1 extra-large egg, lightly beaten

1 cup semisweet chocolate chunks or chocolate chips

¾ cup walnut or pecan pieces

2 baking sheets, greased

makes 24

These are always popular and very hard to beat! Use semisweet chocolate broken up into chunks or a bag of chocolate chips.

classic chocolate chip cookies

Put all the ingredients in a large bowl and mix thoroughly with a wooden spoon. Drop heaping teaspoons of the mixture onto the prepared trays, spacing them well apart.

Bake in a preheated oven at 375°F for 8 to 10 minutes until lightly colored and just firm.

Remove from the oven and let cool on the baking sheets for 2 minutes or until firm enough to transfer to a wire rack. Let cool completely.

Store in an airtight container and eat within 5 days or freeze for up to 1 month.

These cookies have double the chocolate—there's melted chocolate as well as delicious chunks of chocolate.

giant double chocolate nut cookies

Put the chopped chocolate in a heatproof bowl set over a saucepan of barely simmering water and melt gently (do not let the base of the bowl touch the water). Remove the bowl from the heat and let cool.

Meanwhile, using a wooden spoon or electric mixer, beat the butter until creamy. Add the sugars and beat again until light and fluffy. Gradually beat in the egg and vanilla extract, followed by the melted chocolate. Sift the flour, salt, and baking powder into the bowl and stir. When thoroughly mixed, work in the nuts and chocolate chunks. Put heaping tablespoons of the mixture, spaced well apart, onto the prepared baking sheets.

Bake in a preheated oven at 350°F for 12 to 15 minutes until just firm. Remove from the oven and let cool on the trays for 2 minutes or until firm enough to transfer to a wire rack. Let cool completely.

Store in an airtight container and eat within 1 week. The cookies can be frozen for up to 1 month.

5 oz. bittersweet chocolate, chopped

7 tablespoons unsalted butter, at room temperature

⅓ cup sugar

½ cup firmly packed dark brown sugar

1 extra-large egg, beaten

½ teaspoon pure vanilla extract

1 cup all-purpose flour

a pinch of salt

½ teaspoon baking powder

½ cup chopped pecans or walnuts

3½ oz. bittersweet or white chocolate, chopped into chunks

2 baking sheets, greased

makes 16

Brownies are everyone's favorite chocolate indulgence. They're not complicated to make, the most important rule is to aim for the right texture—just set on top, but wonderfully gooey on the inside.

chocolate & cinnamon brownies

½ cup blanched hazelnuts, about 3 oz.

10 oz. bittersweet chocolate

2¼ sticks unsalted butter

3 eggs

1 cup plus 2 tablespoons sugar

½ cup self-rising flour

2 teaspoons ground cinnamon

3 oz. white chocolate chips

a baking pan, 9 x 13 inches, greased and bottom lined with parchment paper

serves 8–12

Put the hazelnuts in a dry skillet and toast over medium heat until aromatic. Do not let them burn. Let cool, then chop them coarsely.

Put the chocolate and butter in a heatproof bowl set over a saucepan of simmering water and melt gently (do not let the base of the bowl touch the water). Remove the bowl from the heat. Put the eggs and sugar in a bowl and beat until pale. Stir in the melted chocolate, flour, cinnamon, chocolate chips, and chopped hazelnuts.

Spoon the mixture into the prepared pan and bake in a preheated oven at 375°F for 30 to 35 minutes until the top is set but the mixture still feels soft underneath. Remove from the oven and let cool in the pan. Serve cut into squares.

blueberry lemon pound cake

2¼ sticks unsalted butter, at room temperature

1¼ cups sugar

grated zest of 1 large unwaxed lemon

4 extra-large eggs, at room temperature

a pinch of salt

1¾ cups self-rising flour

1 cup freeze-dried blueberries or ½ cup soft dried blueberries

confectioners' sugar, for dusting

a daisy cake pan, 11 x 8½ x 2 inches, greased

makes 1 daisy cake

Put the butter in an electric mixer and beat at low speed until creamy. Increase the speed and gradually beat in the sugar, followed by the lemon zest.

Put the eggs and salt in a large measuring cup with a lip, beat lightly, then add to the creamed mixture, 1 tablespoon or so at a time, beating well after each addition. Add 1 tablespoon flour with the last 2 portions of egg to prevent the mixture from separating.

Sift the rest of the flour onto the mixture and gently fold in with a large metal spoon. When you no longer see streaks of flour, mix in the blueberries.

Transfer to the prepared pan and spread evenly. Bake in a preheated oven at 350°F for about 40 minutes or until a skewer inserted in the center comes out clean. Let cool in the pan for 10 minutes, then carefully invert onto a wire rack and let cool completely. Dust with confectioners' sugar before serving.

Store in an airtight container and eat within 5 days.

walnut cake
with coffee syrup

Coffee and walnuts are wonderful together. Drizzling the nutty cake with a spiced coffee syrup leaves it deliciously moist and gooey.

6 eggs, separated (see page 147)

¾ cup sugar

2½ cups walnuts, finely ground in a food processor

¾ cup day-old bread crumbs

whipped cream, to serve

coffee syrup

1¼ cups strong black coffee

½ cup sugar

3 star anise

a springform cake pan, 9 inches diameter, greased and bottom lined with greased parchment paper

serves 8

Put the egg yolks in a large bowl, add ⅔ cup of the sugar and beat until pale. Stir in the ground walnuts and bread crumbs. (The mixture will be very stiff at this stage.)

Beat the egg whites in a separate bowl until soft peaks form, then gradually beat in the remaining sugar. Stir a large spoonful of the beaten egg whites into the cake mixture, then fold in the rest until evenly mixed. Spoon into the prepared cake pan and bake in a preheated oven at 350°F for 35 to 40 minutes, until risen and springy to the touch. Remove from the oven and leave the cake in the pan.

Meanwhile, put the coffee, sugar, and star anise in a saucepan. Heat until the sugar dissolves, then boil for 5 to 6 minutes until syrupy. Let cool slightly.

Using a wooden toothpick, spike the cake all over the surface, then drizzle with half the syrup. Set aside to cool slightly. Serve the cake still warm with lightly whipped cream and the remaining coffee syrup spooned around it in a pool.

yogurt cake

If you don't fancy flavoring this with orange, try something else: cinnamon, honey, vanilla, chocolate, and fruit pieces all work well.

½ cup plain yogurt

1 cup sugar

1½ cups flour

2 eggs

1 tablespoon safflower oil

1 teaspoon baking soda

a pinch of salt

freshly squeezed juice of 1 orange

1 tablespoon confectioners' sugar, to decorate

a deep cake pan, 9 inches diameter, greased

serves 8

Empty the yogurt into a large bowl. Add the sugar, flour, eggs, oil, baking soda, salt, and half the orange juice. Stir well to mix.

Pour the mixture into the prepared cake pan and bake in a preheated oven at 350°F until a knife inserted in the middle comes out clean, 15 to 20 minutes. Remove from the oven and pierce a few holes in the top with a fork. Pour over the remaining orange juice. Let cool slightly, then turn out onto a wire rack to cool.

To decorate, put the confectioners' sugar in a strainer and hold it over the cake. Tap the edge of the strainer to release the sugar, moving around the cake to coat. A very light dusting is sufficient. Serve at room temperature.

french almond cake

I stick unsalted butter, softened

¾ cup sugar

3 extra-large eggs, beaten

I cup slivered almonds, ground in a food processor, plus I tablespoon extra, for sprinkling

⅓ cup self-rising flour

I tablespoon milk or kirsch

confectioners' sugar, for dusting

a cake pan, 8 inches diameter, greased and bottom lined with parchment paper

makes 1 cake

Serve this traditional French cake with tea or coffee, or for dessert with fruit salad, cherries, or berries and cream.

Put the butter, sugar, and eggs in a large bowl, add the ground almonds, flour, and milk, then beat with an electric mixer or whisk. When the mixture is quite light and fluffy, spoon it into the prepared pan and spread evenly. Sprinkle the slivered almonds over the top.

Bake in a preheated oven at 350°F for 30 to 35 minutes or until the cake just springs back when lightly pressed. Run a round-bladed knife around the inside edge of the pan to loosen the cake, then turn out onto a wire rack and let cool. Dust with confectioners' sugar before serving. Store in an airtight container and eat within 5 days.

thanksgiving cranberry bundt

filling

½ cup whole blanched almonds

2 cups fresh cranberries

2 teaspoons ground cinnamon

½ cup firmly packed light brown sugar

batter

I stick unsalted butter, at room temperature

2 extra-large eggs, at room temperature, beaten

I cup firmly packed light brown sugar

I cup sour cream

3 tablespoons finely chopped almonds

2 cups all-purpose flour

I teaspoon ground cinnamon

½ teaspoon baking soda

I teaspoon baking powder

confectioners' sugar for dusting

a cathedral or other Bundt pan, 9 inches diameter, well greased

makes 1 Bundt cake

Make the filling first. Put the almonds in a food processor and chop finely to make a very coarse powder. Transfer to a large bowl. Put the cranberries in the processor and chop coarsely. Add to the almonds, then add the cinnamon and sugar and mix well. Set aside.

To make the batter, put the soft butter, eggs, sugar, sour cream, and chopped almonds in another large bowl. Beat with an electric mixer or whisk on medium speed until very smooth. Sift the flour, cinnamon, baking soda, and baking powder onto the mixture, then stir in with a large metal spoon. When thoroughly blended, spoon half the batter into the prepared pan. Sprinkle the cranberry mixture over the top, then add the rest of the batter.

Bake in a preheated oven at 350°F for about 50 minutes or until a skewer inserted in the thickest part of the cake comes out clean. Let cool in the pan for 15 minutes, then carefully invert onto a wire rack. Dust with confectioners' sugar and let cool completely. Store in an airtight container and eat within 4 days.

Variation Use fresh blueberries instead of cranberries. Make the batter as in the main recipe, but omit the cinnamon and add the grated zest of ½ unwaxed lemon. To make the filling, mix 1½ cups fresh blueberries with ½ cup light brown sugar, ½ cup chopped almonds, and the grated zest of ½ unwaxed lemon. Proceed as in the main recipe.

focaccia

"Focaccia" literally means "a bread that was baked on the hearth," but it is easy to bake in conventional ovens. It is found in many different forms, and can be thin and crisp, thick and soft, round or square. This one is made in a pan, but it can be formed on a baking sheet to any shape you want. A terra cotta bakestone ("testa") or unglazed terra cotta floor tile heated in the oven will give pizzas and "focacce" extra lift and a crisp base. Although a rustic focaccia can be made with any basic pizza dough, the secret of a truly light focaccia lies in three risings, and dimpling the dough with your fingers so it traps olive oil while it bakes. Serve with olive oil, some balsamic vinegar for dipping, and a handful of olives.

5 cups Italian-style flour or all-purpose flour, plus extra for kneading

½ teaspoon fine salt

1½ cakes compressed fresh yeast (for dried yeast, follow the package instructions)

⅔ cup good olive oil

2 cups warm water

coarse sea salt

sprigs of fresh rosemary

2 shallow cake pans, pie or pizza plates, 10 inches diameter, lightly oiled

a water spray

makes 2 thick focacce, 10 inches diameter

Sift the flour and salt into a large bowl and make a hollow in the center. Crumble in the yeast. Pour in 3 tablespoons of the olive oil, then rub in the yeast until the mixture resembles fine bread crumbs. Pour in the warm water and mix with your hands until the dough comes together.

Transfer the dough to a floured surface, wash and dry your hands, and knead for 10 minutes until smooth and elastic. The dough should be quite soft, but if too soft to handle, knead in more flour, 1 tablespoon at a time. Put the dough in a clean, oiled bowl, cover with a damp dish towel or plastic wrap, and let rise in a warm place until doubled in size, 30 minutes to 1½ hours.

Punch down the dough and cut it in half. Put on a floured surface and shape each half into a round ball. Roll out into 2 circles, 10 inches diameter, and put in the pans. Cover with a damp dish towel or plastic wrap and let rise for 30 minutes.

Remove the dish towel and, using your finger tips, make dimples all over the surface of the dough. They can be quite deep. Pour over the remaining oil and sprinkle generously with salt. Cover again and let rise for 30 minutes. Spray with water, sprinkle the rosemary on top, and bake in a preheated oven at 400°F for 20 to 25 minutes. Transfer to a wire rack to cool. Eat the same day or freeze immediately. Serve as bread with a meal, or as a snack with oil, vinegar, and olives as suggested in the recipe introduction.

DRINKS

The idea of throwing a glamorous and sophisticated cocktail party at home might seem a daunting one, but it needn't be. Make sure you have the necessary equipment, such as glasses, cocktail shakers, and barspoons, and enough ingredients to keep the party flowing. Keep things simple by serving just one or two cocktails and always have something exciting for those guests who don't want to drink alcohol.

mojito

Rum is a wonderful base for some great summer cocktails.

5 sprigs of fresh mint
1¾ oz. golden rum
a dash of freshly squeezed lime juice
2 dashes of simple syrup (see note page 172)
crushed ice
club soda, to top up

serves 1

Put the mint in a highball glass, add the rum, lime juice, and simple syrup, and pound with a barspoon until the aroma of the mint is released. Add crushed ice and stir vigorously until the mixture and the mint is spread evenly. Top with club soda and stir again. Serve with straws.

cosmopolitan

This classic cocktail is easy to make and perfect for a crowd.

8 shots of vodka
3 cups cranberry juice
freshly squeezed juice of 4 limes
ice cubes

serves 8

Put all the ingredients in a pitcher and mix. Alternatively, pour the cranberry juice into individual glasses and top with the vodka and lime.

old-fashioned

The delicate mix of sugar and orange zest in the classic Old-Fashioned will bring to life whichever bourbon you choose to use.

1 white sugar cube
2 dashes of orange bitters
1¾ oz. bourbon
ice cubes
a strip of orange zest

serves 1

Put the sugar cube in an old-fashioned glass and pour in the bitters. Muddle the mixture with a barspoon and add a dash of bourbon and a couple of ice cubes. Keep adding ice and bourbon and keep muddling until all the bourbon has been added and the sugar has dissolved. Run orange zest around the rim of the glass, drop it in the glass, and serve.

sea breeze

Any combination of vodka and freshly squeezed juices will work in creating a Breeze to suit your personal taste.

1¾ oz. vodka
ice cubes
5 oz. cranberry juice
1½ oz. fresh grapefruit juice
a wedge of lime

serves 1

Pour the vodka into a highball glass filled with ice. Fill the glass three-quarters full with cranberry juice, and top with fresh grapefruit juice. Garnish with a lime wedge and serve with a straw.

classic martini

The classic martini has evolved, in keeping with social tastes, into the ultra-cold, ultra-dry, mostly vodka-based cocktail enjoyed today.

a dash of vermouth (Noilly Prat or Martini Extra Dry)
2½ oz. well-chilled gin or vodka
an olive or a lemon twist, to garnish

serves 1

Add the vermouth and gin or vodka to a mixing glass filled with ice, and stir. Strain into a frosted martini glass, and garnish with an olive or a lemon twist.

french 75

This drink was named after the big artillery gun that the French used during the First World War.

¾ oz. gin
2 teaspoons freshly squeezed lemon juice
1 teaspoon simple syrup*
chilled champagne, to top up
lemon zest, to garnish

serves 1

Shake the gin, lemon juice, and simple syrup with ice and strain into a champagne flute. Top with champagne and garnish with a long strip of lemon zest.

***Note** To make simple syrup, stir 1 lb. sugar into 1 cup water and bring to a boil, stirring vigorously. Let cool and store in the refrigerator.

margarita

All you need to create a decent margarita is good-quality tequila, limes, and orange-flavored liqueur.

1½ oz. gold tequila
¾ oz. triple sec or Cointreau
freshly squeezed juice of ½ lime
salt, for the glass
cracked ice

serves 1

Shake all the ingredients sharply with cracked ice. Strain into a frosted margarita glass rimmed with salt.

james bond

The James Bond is a variation on the champagne cocktail, using vodka instead of the more traditional brandy.

1 white sugar cube
2 dashes of Angostura bitters
1 oz. vodka
champagne, to top up

serves 1

Put the sugar cube in a champagne flute and moisten with Angostura bitters. Add the vodka and top with champagne.

lemongrass tisane

Tisane is the French word for an infusion of herbs, flowers, or other aromatics.

1–2 fresh red chiles, seeded and sliced
2–4 stalks of lemongrass, outer leaves discarded, inner section thinly sliced
2 inches fresh ginger, peeled and sliced
¼ cup sugar
freshly squeezed juice of 2 lemons

to serve
fresh mint leaves
ice cubes

serves 4

Put the chile in a heatproof bowl with the lemongrass, ginger, and sugar. Add the lemon juice and 1 quart boiling water and stir to dissolve the sugar. Leave to infuse until room temperature.

Strain the cooled liquid and chill for at least 30 minutes. Serve in tall glasses with mint leaves and ice cubes.

orange & apple refresher

2 large oranges, peeled
2 Granny Smith apples
1 inch fresh ginger, peeled
ice cubes, to serve

a juicing machine

serves 2

Push the oranges, apples, and ginger through the juicer. Half-fill 2 tall glasses with ice cubes, pour the juice over the top, and serve.

virgin mary

Since this variation of the Bloody Mary is without vodka, you can go a bit crazy on the spices to compensate.

10 oz. tomato juice
2 grinds of black pepper
2 dashes of Tabasco sauce
2 dashes of Worcestershire sauce
2 dashes of freshly squeezed lemon juice
1 barspoon horseradish sauce
ice cubes
celery stalk, to garnish

serves 1

Shake all the ingredients (except the celery) over ice and strain into a highball filled with ice. Garnish with a celery stalk and serve.

shirley temple

This is a delicious thirst quencher, but only for the very sweet-toothed.

¾ oz. grenadine
ice cubes
ginger ale or lemon soda, to top up
lemon slice, to garnish

serves 1

Pour the grenadine into a highball glass filled with ice and top with either ginger ale or lemon soda. Garnish with a slice of lemon and serve.

RECIPE BASICS

Here you will find all the essential recipes you will need to refer to again and again, such as Broth, Pie Dough, Pizza Dough, Sauces, and Dressings. Many of them can be bought ready-made, but there is nothing like making your own basic recipes to give your final dish the best flavor and that real homemade touch. Most of these recipes can be made in bulk and frozen or refrigerated for future use.

Too many vegetable broths are insipid or taste of a single ingredient. This broth may seem extravagant in its use of vegetables, but will have a very good flavor.

vegetable broth

1 large onion, quartered

2 large carrots, quartered

1 small bunch of celery, coarsely chopped (including leaves)

2 leeks, white parts only, cut in half lengthwise, rinsed and halved again

4 zucchini, thickly sliced

2 tomatoes, cut in half around the center and seeds squeezed out

1 fennel bulb, quartered

1 romaine lettuce heart, coarsely chopped

3 garlic cloves

1 dried red chile

4 bay leaves

a handful of parsley stalks, crushed

½ lemon, sliced

6 black peppercorns

sea salt, to taste

makes 2-3 quarts

Put all the ingredients in a large soup kettle. Add water to cover, about 4 quarts, and bring to a boil. Reduce the heat as soon as it is boiling and simmer for 15 minutes. Stir the broth and skim off the foam, then cook at the barest simmer for 1 hour, skimming often.

Remove from the heat and strain the broth into a bowl through a colander lined with cheesecloth. Discard the contents of the colander after they have cooled. Let the broth cool, then refrigerate for several hours.

At this stage you can reboil the broth to concentrate it, or cover and refrigerate or freeze until needed. The broth will keep in the refrigerator for up to 3 days or can be frozen for up to 6 months.

gravy

This is a thickened gravy for beef which should lightly coat the meat and vegetables.

Put the roasting pan used to cook the meat on top of the stove, heat the reserved 1 tablespoon fat, add the onion, and cook slowly over low heat until browned, about 30 minutes. Do not let it burn. Add the cornstarch and broth mixture, then season to taste with salt and pepper. Stir constantly over low heat until the mixture boils and simmer for a few minutes. Strain it, if you like, or serve it as it is.

1 tablespoon fat from the roasting pan in which the beef or other roast is cooked

1 onion, thinly sliced

1 cup good beef broth, or broth to suit the roast meat or poultry

2 teaspoons cornstarch, mixed with 2 teaspoons cold water

sea salt and freshly ground black pepper

serves 4-6

dijon dressing

A simple all-purpose dressing for salads. For a variation, try whole-grain mustard in place of smooth, and experiment with different vinegars.

1 tablespoon smooth Dijon mustard
1 tablespoon white wine vinegar
¼ cup extra virgin olive oil
1 garlic clove, crushed
sea salt and freshly ground black pepper

serves 4

Put the mustard, vinegar, oil, and garlic in a bowl and mix with a fork or small metal whisk. Add enough water for the consistency you want—1 to 2 tablespoons—and salt and black pepper to taste.

horseradish sauce

Grating the horseradish will make your eyes water, but the result is worth it.

1 large horseradish root
1 tablespoon white wine vinegar
1 cup heavy cream
sea salt

makes 2-2½ cups, serves 6-8

Scrape the fresh horseradish root clean and grate it finely to give 2 tablespoons.

Put in a bowl, add the vinegar and salt, and stir well. Add the cream and beat until it becomes thick and light. Let it rest at room temperature for at least 2 hours, but serve the same day.

red onion marmalade

Delicious on burgers, with sausages and cold meat, or on bruschetta with goat cheese.

2 tablespoons olive oil
1½ lb. red onions, very thinly sliced
1 bay leaf
1 teaspoon fresh thyme leaves
¼ cup firmly packed soft brown sugar
3 tablespoons balsamic vinegar
⅔ cup red wine
grated zest and juice of 1 unwaxed orange
sea salt and freshly ground black pepper

serves 8

Heat the oil in a large saucepan until hot. Add the onions, bay leaf, and thyme and salt and pepper to taste. Cover with a lid and cook over low heat, stirring occasionally, for 30 minutes until the onions are softened and translucent.

Add the sugar, vinegar, red wine, and the orange zest and juice. Cook uncovered for a further 1½ hours until no liquid is left and the onions are a dark, rich, red. Stir frequently during the last 30 minutes to stop the onions burning.

Let the mixture cool, then transfer to sterilized jars (see page 4). It will keep refrigerated for several weeks.

chile oil

1¼ cups extra virgin olive oil
4 dried red chiles, coarsely chopped

makes 1¼ cups

Put the oil and chiles in a screw-top bottle and leave to infuse for 2 days before using.

pâte brisée

Sift the flour and salt together onto a sheet of wax paper.

Put the butter and egg yolk in a food processor and blend until smooth. Add the water and blend again. Add the flour and salt and pulse until just mixed.

Transfer to a lightly floured work surface and knead gently until smooth. Form into a ball, flatten slightly and wrap in plastic wrap. Chill in the refrigerator for at least 30 minutes. Let the dough return to room temperature before rolling out.

Baking blind Line the tart crust with foil, parchment paper, or all-purpose plastic wrap (flicking the edges inward toward the center so that they don't catch on the crust), then fill with baking beans. Set on a baking sheet and bake blind in the center of a preheated oven at 400°F for 10 to 12 minutes. Remove the foil, parchment paper, or plastic wrap and the baking beans and return the pie crust to the oven for a further 5 to 7 minutes to dry out completely.

2 cups all-purpose flour

1 teaspoon salt

9 tablespoons unsalted butter, softened

1 extra-large egg yolk

2½–3 tablespoons ice water

makes about 14 oz.

american pie crust dough

This is a recipe for the classic American pie crust. It is a very light, crumbly crust when baked—similar to shortcrust and with a real homemade feeling. The quantity is enough for two pies. You could make and bake both pies now or freeze all the dough to use later.

Sift the flour and salt into a large bowl. Cut in the shortening using 2 round-bladed knives or a pastry blender (or do this in a food processor).

Put the egg in a separate bowl. Stir in the vinegar or lemon juice, then add the water.

Pour the wet mixture into the dry mixture, then cut it in with the knives or pastry blender.

Bring the dough together quickly, using your hands. Knead until smooth, either in the bowl or on a lightly floured work surface. Divide in 2 so it is easier to roll out later. Shape the 2 balls of dough into flattened balls, wrap in plastic wrap, then chill for at least 30 minutes before rolling out.

2¾ cups all-purpose flour, plus extra for dusting

a good pinch of salt

1⅓ cups vegetable shortening, chilled

1 egg, beaten

1 tablespoon wine vinegar or lemon juice

¼ cup ice water

makes about 1½ lb. pastry dough, enough for 2 single deep pie crusts, 9 inches diameter

These Yorkshire puddings can be made individually,
or make one big one and cut it into pieces to serve.

yorkshire pudding

1 cup plus 1 tablespoon milk

2 eggs

¾ cup all-purpose flour

½ teaspoon salt

4–6 tablespoons fat from the roasting pan

1 small roasting pan, 18 x 12 inches, a 6-cup muffin pan, or a 12-cup pan

serves 6

Put the milk, eggs, flour, and salt in a bowl and beat well.

Heat the fat on top of the stove in 1 large pan or divide between 6 cups (1 tablespoon fat each) or 12 cups (½ teaspoon fat). Pour in the batter (take care because it will spatter).

Cook in a preheated oven at 450°F until well risen (35 minutes for the large pan or 15 minutes for the individual pans). Serve as soon as possible.

For a really good pizza dough, try to use the Italian "00" flour,
which you can buy in Italian stores and large supermarkets.
Otherwise, choose an ordinary all-purpose flour.

pizza dough

To make the dough, put the semolina flour in the bowl of a food mixer fitted with a dough hook attachment or a food processor with a plastic blade. Crumble the fresh yeast into the flour, add a generous pinch of salt and the lemon juice, then work in the olive oil and enough of the warm water to form a very soft dough.

Remove from the bowl and transfer to a floured surface. Knead for 10 minutes or until the dough is smooth and elastic. Put the dough in a clean, oiled bowl (or an oiled plastic bag), cover, and let rise until doubled in size (about 1 hour). Use as directed in the pizza recipe on page 72.

1⅔ cups fine Italian semolina flour (*farina di semola*)

½ cake compressed fresh yeast

a pinch of salt

1 tablespoon freshly squeezed lemon juice

1 tablespoon olive oil

about 1¼ cups warm water

makes 2 thin-crust pizzas, 8-10 inches diameter

sources

KITCHENWARE

Anthropologie
375 West Broadway
New York, NY 10012
www.anthropologie.com
These loft-like stores sell affordable home items with that Euro-flea-market style.

Bed, Bath & Beyond
620 Avenue of the Americas
New York, NY 10011
tel: 212-255-3550
www.bedbathandbeyond.com
Large-scale department store with everything for the home.

Bridge Kitchenware
711 3rd Avenue
New York, NY 10022
tel: 212-688-4220
www.bridgekitchenware.com
Imported professional-grade kitchenware for the home gourmet cook.

The Container Store
tel: 888-266-8246
www.containerstore.com
Stocks an exceptional mix of storage and organizational products. Everything you need to get your kitchen ready for cooking. Locations nationwide.

Crate & Barrel
tel: 800-967-6696
www.crateandbarrel.com
Good-value china, glass, and plastic containers. Locations nationwide. Mail order. Catalog.

Dean & Deluca
560 Broadway
New York, NY 10012
tel: 212-226-6800
www.deandeluca.com

A wide selection of kitchenware, gifts, gourmet foods, wines, cookbooks, and recipes. See web site for the location nearest you.

Michael C. Fina
545 5th Avenue
New York, NY 10017
tel: 212-557-2500
www.michaelcfina.com
New York's premier retail source of fine china, crystal, tableware, flatware, and home furnishings.

Fishs Eddy
889 Broadway
New York, NY 10011
tel: 212-420-2090
www.fishseddy.com
Specializing in American sturdyware–including dinnerware, flatware, and glassware. A wide selection of vintage dishware, but designer selections are also available.

Garnet Hill
279 Main Street
Franconia, NH 03580
tel: 800-870-3513
www.garnethill.com
Colorful housewares and accessories, such as placemats, table linens, and pepper mills.

Global Table
107–109 Sullivan Street
New York, NY 10012
tel: 212-431-5839
www.globaltable.com
Beautiful, interesting, and useful objects for eating and drinking, such as tableware, glassware, vases, trays, and utensils.

Ikea
tel: 800-434-IKEA
www.ikea.com
Affordable kitchenware. Locations nationwide.

Linens 'n' Things
tel: 866-568-7378
www.lnt.com
Large specialty retailer of home textiles, housewares, and decorative accessories. Locations nationwide.

Le Magasin
408 North Clark Street
Chicago, IL 60610
tel: 312-396-0030
Beautiful tableware and antiques store offering tableware lines recreated from archival patterns.

Pacific Rim Gourmet
tel: 800-910-9657
www.pacificrim-gourmet.com
The ultimate on-line source for hard-to-find kitchenware, such as woks, bamboo steamers, clay pots, rich baskets, sushi supplies, and more.

Pier One Imports
tel: 800-245-4595
www.pier1.com
A specialty retailer offering furniture and home accessories with a distinctive international flavor.

Porte Rouge
1911 W. Division
Chicago, IL 60622
tel: 773-269-2800
www.porterouge.biz
Offers an excellent collection of high-end porcelain, specialty kitchenware, and hand-painted ceramics from Provence, as well lots of other affordable options.

Pottery Barn
tel: 888-779-5176
www.potterybarn.com
An excellent source of stylish, affordable homewares, expertly displayed in-store to offer inspiration. Locations nationwide.

Sur La Table
1996 West Gray
Houston, TX 77019-4808
tel: 713-533-0400
www.surlatable.com
Offers a wide range of kitchen products including copper cookware, books, linens, bakeware, knives, electrical appliances, and gadgets. Locations nationwide.

Takashimaya
693 5th Avenue
New York, NY 10022
tel: 212-350-0100
Japanese department store offering a wide selection of kitchenware, tableware, and accessories for the home.

Target
tel: 888-304-4000
www.target.com
Department store delivering today's best retail trends at affordable prices. Locations nationwide.

Terence Conran Shop
407 E 59th Street
New York, NY 10022
tel: 212-755-9079
The British design guru's home-furnishings emporium, offering everything from linens to kitchen- and tableware.

Urban Outfitters
tel: 800-959-8794
www.urbanoutfitters.com
Locations nationwide.
Affordably priced rugs, sheets, table trays, kitchenware, and kitschy home accessories.

Williams-Sonoma
tel: 877-812-6235
www.williams-sonoma.com
A leading specialty retailer of goods for well-appointed kitchens.

SPECIALTY FOOD STORES

Beekman Liquors
500 Lexington Avenue
New York, NY 10017
tel: 212-759-5857
www.beekmanliquors.com
Specialists in fine Bordeaux, single malt Scotch whiskies, ports, high-quality Californian wines as well as a wide variety of other wines and liquors.

Kalustyan's
123 Lexington Avenue
New York, NY 10016
tel: 212-685-3451
www.kalustyans.com
A landmark store carrying fine specialty foods such as spices, herbs, candies, coffee, tea, and healthy snacks, plus unique cookware and accessories.

Kitchen/Market
218 Eighth Avenue
New York, NY 10011
tel: 888-468-4433
www.kitchenmarket.com
Specialty food store that offers high-quality, unique ingredients from around the world. Also carries a growing selection of hand-picked gifts from Latin America and Southeast Asia.

Whole Foods Market
www.wholefoodsmarket.com
The world's largest retailer of natural and organic foods. Locations nationwide.

index

conversion charts

Weights and measures have been rounded up or down slightly to make measuring easier.

VOLUME EQUIVALENTS:

American	Metric	Imperial
1 teaspoon	5 ml	
1 tablespoon	15 ml	
1/4 cup	60 ml	2 fl.oz.
1/3 cup	75 ml	2 1/2 fl.oz.
1/2 cup	125 ml	4 fl.oz.
2/3 cup	150 ml	5 fl.oz. (1/4 pint)
3/4 cup	175 ml	6 fl.oz.
1 cup	250 ml	8 fl.oz.

WEIGHT EQUIVALENTS:

Imperial	Metric
1 oz.	25 g
2 oz.	50 g
3 oz.	75 g
4 oz.	125 g
5 oz.	150 g
6 oz.	175 g
7 oz.	200 g
8 oz. (1/2 lb.)	250 g
9 oz.	275 g
10 oz.	300 g
11 oz.	325 g
12 oz.	375 g
13 oz.	400 g
14 oz.	425 g
15 oz.	475 g
16 oz. (1 lb.)	500 g
2 lb.	1 kg

MEASUREMENTS:

Inches	Cm
1/4 inch	5 mm
1/2 inch	1 cm
3/4 inch	1.5 cm
1 inch	2.5 cm
2 inches	5 cm
3 inches	7 cm
4 inches	10 cm
5 inches	12 cm
6 inches	15 cm
7 inches	18 cm
8 inches	20 cm
9 inches	23 cm
10 inches	25 cm
11 inches	28 cm
12 inches	30 cm

OVEN TEMPERATURES:

110°C	(225°F)	Gas 1/4
120°C	(250°F)	Gas 1/2
140°C	(275°F)	Gas 1
150°C	(300°F)	Gas 2
160°C	(325°F)	Gas 3
180°C	(350°F)	Gas 4
190°C	(375°F)	Gas 5
200°C	(400°F)	Gas 6
220°C	(425°F)	Gas 7
230°C	(450°F)	Gas 8
240°C	(475°F)	Gas 9

recipe credits

LAURA WASHBURN trained at the prestigious Paris cooking school, Ecole de Cuisine La Varenne, and worked with Patricia Wells, author of *A Food Lover's Guide to Paris.*

Bacon, avocado, and feta salad
Beef provençal
Braised pork chops with tomato, orange, and chile
Bulghur wheat pilaff
Butternut squash with pistou
Carrots with cream and herbs
Chicken, asparagus, and gorgonzola salad with hazelnuts
Chili with all the trimmings
Duck breasts with peppercorns
French beans with garlic
French fries
French onion soup
Greek omelet
Lemon-spiced chicken
Linguine, peas, pancetta, and sage
Macaroni gratin
Meatballs in red bell pepper sauce
Moroccan shrimp with couscous
Mussels with fennel, tomatoes, garlic, and saffron
Sole meunière
Peach Cobbler
Pork chops with piquant sauce
Potato wedges
Rice pudding
Ricotta cake
Rustic pâté with green peppercorns
Savoy cabbage with bacon and cream
Spring lamb stew with vegetables
Tomato salad with anchovy vinaigrette
Whole roast monkfish
Yogurt cake

LOUISE PICKFORD is a British food writer, now living and working in Sydney. She writes for several magazines and has written a number of cookbooks.

Baked eggs with smoked salmon
Charred asparagus and herb frittata
Chicken "panini" with mozzarella
Chilled lemongrass tisane
Chile oil
Chile-spiked cornbread
Chocolate and cinnamon brownies
Cinnamon-soaked granola
Creamy eggs with arugula pesto
Eggs benedict
Fresh figs with ricotta and

honeycomb
Hash browns with sausages
Mushrooms on toast with cheese
Orange and apple refresher
Pan-fried steak with horseradish and chive butter
Peppered tuna with salsa rossa
Prosciutto-wrapped pork
Shrimp fried rice
Shrimp with chile oil
Tex-Mex ribs
Tomato pizza with capers and anchovies
Waffles with maple syrup ice cream
Walnut cake with coffee syrup

LESLEY WATERS is one of the best-known television chefs and teacher-cooks in Britain. She is a star of TV cooking on the BBC's *Ready Steady Cook.*

Bitter chocolate and orange muffins
Bloody Mary
Classic creamy mashed potato
Coq au vin
Dijon dressing
Green Thai vegetable curry
Lamb steaks with coriander cumin crust
Mediterranean fish stew
Pan-grilled bruschetta with onion marmalade and goat cheese
Peppered goat cheese
Peppered sage pork with pasta
Pizza topping suggestions
Red onion marmalade
Roasted potatoes
Seared peppered beef salad
Seared scallops with brittle prosciutto
Seared swordfish with avocado and salsa
Tropical smoothie
Very berry smoothie
Warm chunky salmon pâté
Whole-grain mustard tarragon chicken
Whole roasted chicken

MAXINE CLARK teaches at Alastair Little's Tasting Places in Sicily and Tuscany. Her work appears regularly in magazines.

American pie crust dough
Apple tart
Foccacia
Gorgonzola and ricotta risotto
Grilled salmon fillets
Italian mixed salad
Lasagne
Pâte brisée
Pizza dough
Pumpkin pie
Salmon, dill, and Parmesan tart

Tiramisu
Traditional New York cheesecake
Vegetable broth

FRAN WARDE trained as a chef and ran a successful restaurant, and catering business. She is now a freelance food writer.

Beef en croûte with mustard sauce
Cosmopolitan
Making coffee
Making the perfect cup of tea
Mashed minty potatoes and peas
Onion tart with tomato salsa
Raspberries in champagne gelatin
Risotto primavera
Salade niçoise
Smoked fish chowder
Smoked wild salmon and scrambled eggs with avruga
Spicy-crust roasted rack of lamb
Steak and tomato sandwich

BEN REED was named Cocktail Bartender of the Year in 1997 in a competition sponsored by Absolut Vodka.

Classic Martini
French 75
James Bond
Margarita
Mojito
Old-fashioned
Sea breeze
Shirley Temple
Virgin Mary

LINDA COLLISTER'S books on baking have sold over 500,000 copies worldwide.

Blueberry lemon pound cake
Chocolate chip cookies
French almond cake
Giant double chocolate nut cookies
Mississippi mud pie
Thanksgiving cranberry bundt

SONIA STEVENSON is one of Britain's great chefs. She often appears on TV, and is a judge on BBC's *Masterchef.*

Gravy
Horseradish sauce
Roast beef
Traditional fish pie
Tuna with paprika crumbs
Yorkshire puddings

CLARE FERGUSON has been the Food Editor of *Elle* and *She* magazines and is the author of many books.

Apricot and orange gelato
Bitter chocolate and hazelnut gelato
Eggplant antipasto with pine nuts
Penne with mozzarella
Spanish potato omelet

CELIA BROOKS BROWN is one of the talented teacher-chefs at the bookshop, Books For Cooks, in Notting Hill, London.

Blueberry muffins
Pancakes
Raspberry roulade
Tuscan panzanella

LINDY WILDSMITH is well known from her appearances in the celebrity kitchen at *House & Garden* fairs. She also has her own cooking school.

Quick Neapolitan tomato sauce
Ragù
Spaghetti alla carbonara
Spaghetti with baby clams

JANE NORAIKA is head chef at London's most celebrated vegetarian restaurant, *Food for Thought.*

Leek, feta, and black olive tart
Roasted vegetable dauphinois

LINDA TUBBY is a leading London food writer and food stylist. Her work appears in a number of magazines.

Hake in green sauce
Oysters rockefeller

MANISHA GAMBHIR HARKINS is Features Editor of *The Master's Table* magazine and was the Guild of Food Writers' Food Journalist of the Year in 1999.

Butternut squash soup with allspice and pine nuts